HAUNTED HILLSBOROUGH COUNTY

HAUNTED HILLSBOROUGH COUNTY

ERIC STANWAY

Haunted America

Published by Haunted America
A Division of The History Press
Charleston, SC 29403
www.historypress.net

First published 2014

Manufactured in the United States

ISBN 978.1.60949.324.6

Library of Congress CIP data applied for.

Notice: The information in this book is true and complete to the best of our knowledge. It is offered without guarantee on the part of the author or The History Press. The author and The History Press disclaim all liability in connection with the use of this book.

CONTENTS

ACKNOWLEDGEMENTS

Obviously, a book such as this one is not written in a vacuum. Accordingly, I would like to thank a number of people without whose help its production would not have been possible.

I am indebted to the following: Susan Clark of Souhegan Paranormal Investigators; Fiona Broome of Hollow Hills; Eric Perry of the Central New Hampshire Paranormal Society; Theresa Harlow-Sillanpaa, director and founder of the Conscious Spirit Paranormal Group; T.J. Swick of SilentWhispers Paranormal Group; the staff at the Country Tavern in Amherst; the staff of the Common Man Restaurant in Amherst; Loretta Jackson of the Cabinet Press; the staff at the North Eastern Paranormal Society; Christopher Balzano at www.masscrossroads.com; April Sheerin of the New Millennium Psychic Center; Francestown resident B.J. Carbee; Anita Creager, president of the Merrimack Historical Society; Wilton resident and artist Gail Hoar; and Wilton resident and author Robin Ross Schoen.

Last but certainly not least, my thanks to The History Press commissioning editor Katie Orlando for putting up with me.

1

DUNSTABLE AND MONSON

THE ROOTS OF HILLSBOROUGH COUNTY

Let me tell you a few things about New England.

Now, since moving to this country from England back in the mid-1960s, I've been witness to a lot of different aspects of this great nation. I've seen the Rocky Mountains, spent time among the mighty redwoods of California, ridden through the deserts of New Mexico and Arizona and traveled through the swamps of Georgia, North Carolina and Arkansas. All of these places had their own tales to tell. But when it comes to downright flinty spookiness, New England has almost all of them beat. (I shall, of course, except the great cities of Richmond, Virginia, and New Orleans, Louisiana, the paranormal aspects of which cannot be denied.)

But there's something singular about this part of the country. Maybe it has to do with those stern Puritans who settled the land back in the seventeenth century, fighting the Native Americans to gain a foothold in the earth.

Perhaps those people brought their own ghosts with them from the Old Country, promulgating their ancient superstitions in these adopted lands. For whatever reason, spirits abide here, in every forgotten road, stone wall and ancient cellar hole. Since I adopted this profession of digging out forgotten history, I have developed the habit of looking through my car window at forgotten dwellings; seeking out arcane, disused roads; and talking to many of the old-timers who have regaled me with endless tales of spectral visitations. Believe me—ghosts walk here, and their numbers are legion.

As I write this in December 2013, a thick snow is falling on the scenery outside. There is little sound to be heard; only a few hardy travelers are

Outline map of Hillsborough County. *From* The History of Hillsborough County, *by Duane Hamilton Hurd, 1885.*

heading out on these treacherous roads. Many of them are ending up in ditches, waiting for the tow trucks to help them out of their dilemmas. For the most part, though, things are quiet, as all sound is muffled by the ancient shroud of winter's wrath. Right down the road from where I live, an odd tale has been passed down through the generations of a young girl who, destitute and desperate, abandoned her child in the frozen wastes.

A full account of the tragedy was published in the March 15, 1866 edition of the *New Hampshire Sentinel*:

> *The name of the girl is Alfaretta Boyce, not quite 18 years of age. She has another illegitimate child, about five years old, born when she was but thirteen years old. She had brothers and sisters, and a poor, infirm mother, who was a widow. It seems that on Monday, the 5th inst., that bleak, cold day, with the thermometer at zero, Alfaretta got out of the cars at Fitzwilliam depot with her child in her arms, returning from a visit to a distant town, where the child was born. She immediately started on foot to Howville, a village about three miles distant in a southerly direction, where a number of her relatives live. She proceeded not more than a hundred rods, before she came to a piece of woods by the road side. There she stopped and turned directly into the woods, eight or ten rods, and then stripped the child of all its clothing, and put upon it a thin summer frock, tied her handkerchief firmly around its head so as to cover the mouth, that its cries might not be heard by passers on the road; and then laid her baby down on the ground in a thicket, and left it to die! Heart, harder than the nether millstone, possessed by a girl hardly 18 years of age! Who has the heart to plead for such a remorseless mother as this?*

When Alfaretta arrived at her destination, her alarmed relatives sent out a search party to seek the missing baby. They eventually discovered the infant, but it was so frozen into the earth that they literally had to pry it from the ground. Upon her arrest, she was heard to say, "They cannot but hang me fast enough."

I have brought up this tale to illustrate the harsh nature of this area throughout the eighteenth and nineteenth centuries. Deprivation and violence were the norm in these parts, and early settlers had an extremely difficult time wresting a living out of this cold, rocky land.

THE TYNG FAMILY

Of all the counties in New Hampshire, Hillsborough is the largest and most populous. Officially incorporated in 1769, it was named after Wills Hill, the First Marquess of Downshire (May 30, 1718–October 7, 1793). He was known as the Viscount Hillsborough from 1742 to 1751 and the Earl of Hillsborough from 1751 to 1789.

The southern part of the county has its roots in the ancient and venerable district of Dunstable township. This was an enormous tract of land, involving thousands of acres, and was one of the earliest settled portions of this part of New England.

The township was founded by Edward Tyng, who was born in Dunstable, England, in 1610. He arrived in New England in 1639, along with his brother, William; settled on the banks of the Merrimack River; and promptly purchased three thousand acres, which he named after his hometown. His brother, meanwhile, was buying up land in what is now Braintree, Massachusetts, and became a very rich man.

These three thousand acres would prove to be the seed that would birth a great oak, primarily due to the misfortune of the local tribes. This story centers on Passaconway, sachem of the Pennacook tribe, who in time became *bashaba*, or chief of chiefs, and held sway over a loose conglomeration of tribes that had gathered together to protect themselves against the Mohawks.

Passaconaway. *From* The History of Manchester, Formerly Derryfield, in New Hampshire: Including that of Ancient Amoskeag, or the Middle Merrimack Valley; Together with the Address, Poem, and Other Proceedings, of the Centennial Celebration, of the Incorporation of Derryfield; at Manchester, October 22, 1851, *by Chandler Eastman Potter, 1856.*

Passaconaway had three children—a girl and two boys, Nanamocomuck, the sachem of Wachusetts, and Wonnalancet. Of what we know of these brothers, they exhibited extremely different temperaments. Nanamocomuck was the more hot-headed of the two, while Wonnalancet's name bespeaks his character; the sobriquet has two parts: *Wonne*, meaning "pleasant," and *Nangshonat*, meaning "to breathe." His friendship with the settlers gained him considerable distrust among the neighboring tribes.

At a young age, Nanamocomuck became sachem of the Wachusetts and, for a time, was as amenable to the newcomers as his father; as time went on, however, he began to develop an understandable animosity toward the newcomers.

Trouble erupted on February 13, 1656, when Nanamocomuck and two other tribesmen, Quaquinsheman and

Momackecomock, were summoned before Middlesex Court due to an outstanding debt of twenty-five pounds and ten shillings, owed to an English trader by the name of John Tinker. The court ordered that half of the sum should be paid in four months and the remainder at the end of nine months.

A year later, the debt was still unpaid, and Nanamocomuck and Momackecomock were again hauled into court on a total outstanding debt of forty-two pounds, seventeen shillings and two pence. Although this debt had been incurred by Momackecomock, the responsibility for it fell to Nanamocomuck, as sachem of the tribe. Consequently, he was thrown into prison.

Upon learning of his son's incarceration, Passaconaway fell into a deep depression, and his other son, Wonnalancet, was forced into the unenviable position of either letting his brother rot in jail or selling off the tribe's property to settle the debt. This was an island known as Wickasaucke, situated in the middle of the Merrimack River. The sale was finalized on November 8, 1649, and a large portion of the land was handed over to the Europeans. The remainder of the island was sold off in 1665, whereupon Nanamocomuck, embittered by his long imprisonment, decided he'd had about enough of the white men and scooted off to Maine. There, he took up residence with the Amariscoggins, as this tribe owed a certain amount of fealty to his father.

Edward Tyng ended up purchasing the rest of the land and built a large mansion in what is now Tyngsborough, Massachusetts. He felt so badly about how he had acquired the property, however, that he permitted Wonnalancet to live in his house, where the old man would spend days sitting on a massive boulder, gazing out at his tribe's lost homeland.

We move along to August 1724, when Edward's great-grandson John Alford Tyng was born. John was, to put it mildly, not a very nice individual. In time, he became attracted to a young girl by the name of Judith Thompson, whose father, Ezra, was a prominent local citizen. Judith, known to be one of the most beautiful women in New England, would help out at the Tyng mansion when the family hosted parties.

In order to realize his lecherous desires, Tyng employed the services of one Dr. Blood, a notorious conman and drunkard. Blood posed as a minister and presided over a wedding of extremely dubious circumstances.

It appears that the Tyng family wasn't aware of this marriage, and John moved his new wife to another house in Dunstable, where she bore him two children. When, however, she became pregnant with a third in 1771, something went horribly wrong.

The Tyng mansion, photographed in 1934. *Historic American Buildings Survey Photos, Library of Congress.*

It was at this point that John Alford Tyng evidently began entertaining homicidal thoughts about his wife and children. When it came to execution, however, it seems that he just didn't have the nerve. Accordingly, he employed Dr. Blood again—this time to murder his entire family.

Legend tells us that John invited Dr. Blood into his house, whereupon he butchered Judith and the children while her husband cowered in the next room. They were then buried under the fireplace.

In order to cover up his family's disappearance, John concocted the story that they had gone to visit relatives in Boston. In sympathy, his father, Eleazar, invited him to move into the familial home. Dr. Blood had gone on his way, and everyone seemed to be buying John's alibi. To all extents, John must have felt he had gotten away with murder.

What he hadn't counted on was Judith. She was back—and out for revenge.

The first victim of Judith's wrath was, quite naturally, Dr. Blood. Drunk, as usual, he was walking down a quiet country road, occupied by what is now Route 101 in Amherst, New Hampshire. Suddenly, he heard footsteps behind him. Turning about, he saw there was nobody there. It was probably at this point that he began running for his life. Dr. Blood pitched to the ground, and the ceramic liquor bottle he carried in his front pocket broke under his weight. A puddle formed on the earth, and Dr. Blood literally drowned in his own drink. When the body was discovered the next morning, the imprint of a woman's shoe was found imbedded in the back of his head.

When John Tyng got word of his associate's demise, he went completely off the rails. He knew that Judith was exacting vengeance, and he was probably next. Trying to shake off the specter, he spent the next four years moving to a number of different residences, but she was always right behind him.

As he moved into his third house, John became more and more isolated. His family attempted to visit him but were turned away by Judith's ghost. As they had no idea that they were looking at a spirit, they simply assumed that the girl was hostile to their interests.

Finally, in desperation, they turned to an old family friend, Captain Joseph Butterfield, and implored him to visit the sick man. When Butterfield arrived at the house, Judith answered the door and tried to force him from the home. Undeterred, he ran upstairs to John's bedroom, where he found the dying man in his last throes. At that moment, Judith materialized in the room and addressed her husband, telling him that, for the rest of time, his name would be forgotten. John sat up in bed to address the spirit, but the effort killed him.

As it turned out, Judith's prediction turned out to be largely true. John Alford Tyng's name disappeared from his grave almost immediately. When the stone was replaced, the inscription would vanish yet again. It was only after the date of death was altered from 1775 to 1771—the year that Judith and her children were butchered—that the notation remained intact. According to legend, John Tyng's remains are not really interred under the stone; as a matter of fact, nobody really seems to know where they are.

John Alford Tyng's grave in present-day Tyngsborough, Massachusetts. *Photograph by the author.*

Over the years, as the Tyng mansion became vacant, it began to develop a reputation as a haunted house. According to Fiona Broom, there is a story from the nineteenth

The Tyng family burial ground, adjacent to the ruins of the old mansion. *Photograph by the author.*

Edward Tyng's grave in the Tyng family burial ground. *Souhegan Paranormal Investigators.*

An etching of the Merrimack River. *From the* Granite Bay Monthly, *March 1884.*

century concerning a young man who, along with his valet, sought refuge at the mansion during a particularly horrendous storm.

Upon knocking on the front door, he was greeted by a woman in a green dress. Behind her, he could perceive there was a large party going on. He explained his situation and requested that his horse and valet stay in the barn overnight while he took shelter in the house.

The young woman readily assented to his requests and invited him to join the others at the party. He protested that he was extremely tired and, with her permission, would take a light supper and then repair directly to bed.

The man spent a fitful night as the storm continued to rage outside. Finally, he fell into a deep slumber.

Upon awakening the next morning, he was astonished to discover that the room had undergone a complete metamorphosis. The wallpaper was hanging in strips from the walls, and a thick layer of dust covered all of the furniture. He went to explore the rest of the house, only to discover that every portion of it was similarly dilapidated. He ran into his valet, who informed him that the barn was in a similar condition.

The Tyng mansion is gone now, a victim to an arsonist who burned it to the ground in 1979. All that remains are the front steps and lawn, as the rest of the site is a parking lot. Just a short walk away, however, is the Tyng burial ground, a haven for restless spirits. Edward Tyng is said to still walk here. There have also been reports of people seeing the spirit of Wonalancet, still sitting on a huge glacial boulder, gazing out on what had once been the home of his people.

The remains of a wall that once stood in front of the site of the Tyng mansion in present-day Tyngsborough, Massachusetts. *Photograph by the author.*

Above: A close shot of the front steps that originally stood in front of the Tyng mansion. *Photograph by the author.*

Below: A strange mist hovering over the Tyng burial ground, photographed by the Souhegan Paranormal Investigators on October 21, 2009. *Souhegan Paranormal Investigators.*

A strange mist emanating from the front steps of the Tyng mansion, photographed by the Souhegan Paranormal Investigators on October 21, 2009. *Souhegan Paranormal Investigators.*

Notable by her absence is Judith Thompson herself. It has been reported that she now haunts a private house in Nashua. The residents there claim that she is a benign spirit that makes an excellent babysitter.

Border Troubles

In its earliest years, the boundary lines of Hillsborough County were in constant dispute. According to a chapter in *The History of Hillsborough*, written in 1885 by one George M. Ramsdell, Massachusetts had claimed that

> *the division boundary between that state and New Hampshire was defined by a line drawn from the Atlantic coast three miles north of the mouth of the Merrimack River, and running on the northerly and easterly side of the river, and at a distance of three miles from it, to a point three miles beyond the*

> *parallel of the junction of the Winnipiseogee and the Pemmigewassett; thence due west to the Connecticut. This covered all the territory included in the present limits of the county of Hillsborough, excepting the towns of Pelham and such portion of the town of Hudson as lies more than three miles from the Merrimack River. It also included the whole of Cheshire County and the larger part of the present limits of Merrimack and Sullivan Counties.*

This is where things get a bit fuzzy. New Hampshire had a slightly different opinion about where the boundary lay. By its reasoning, the towns of Pelham, Hudson, Litchfield, Nashua, Merrimack, Hollis and Amherst, and all of the other towns fourteen miles from the latitude, were actually part of Massachusetts. In particular, the huge, ancient township of Dunstable, comprising some two hundred square miles, was included in the county of Middlesex, Massachusetts.

In about 1740, the British king, George II, decided to settle the issue of the disputed boundaries once and for all. He rewrote the boundaries and acceded a considerable amount of land to New Hampshire. This from *The History of Hillsborough*:

> *Previous to 1740 a board of commissioners, acting under royal authority, had established the eastern boundary, but failing to agree upon the southern line the King himself terminated the controversy in favor of New Hampshire, fixing the present boundary and granting the State a much larger territory than had been claimed. The decision, though somewhat arbitrary and not in accordance with the prayer of either party, was founded upon sound suggestions. By the letter of the grant to Massachusetts it would seem that her claim was good, but it was urged by the King's Council that when the Massachusetts grant was made the country was unexplored, and the course of the Merrimack was supposed to be substantially at right angles with the ocean its entire length, and that it would be just and equitable between the parties to follow as its general course was from the west to the coast and no further.*

Well, the people living in the affected towns were not terribly thrilled by this turn of events. For one thing, Massachusetts had a considerable amount of resources not available to its northern neighbor, including well-armed garrisons that could dispel the still-constant threats by tribes of marauding Indians. New Hampshire, by contrast, was a relatively unarmed province, and it was felt by many that this move was putting its settlers' lives in mortal danger.

THE GHOST TOWN OF MONSON

Many small towns suffered during these perilous times, and some actually ended up disappearing altogether. One notable example is the ghost town of Monson, which straddles the border of what are now Milford and Hollis. A rare example of an extinct eighteenth-century community, Monson can still be seen to this day, a collection of ancient cellar holes, old disused roads and one restored house.

The town was founded on the patch of land encompassed by Muddy Brook and the Souhegan River, encompassing about seventeen thousand acres.

Although a town charter was granted on April 4, 1746, things were never particularly promising for the nascent settlement.

As a matter of fact, Monson existed for only twenty-four years.

You can still see Monson and conjure up life in those wild and woolly times. Thanks in no small part to local residents Russ and the late Geri Dickerman, the town still exists, deep in the woods, with old horse and cow trails weaving their way past collapsing ancient cellar holes.

The Gault House in Monson, New Hampshire. Restored in 1998, this is the only standing building in the town. *Photograph by the author.*

The remains of William Nevins's house in the ghost town of Monson, New Hampshire. *Photograph by the author.*

There are presently seven cellar holes in Monson Center. Early census reports indicate that about fifteen families lived there at one point, raising the probability that a large portion of the populace was occupying tents. Monson was actually the first inland settlement in New Hampshire; the earliest settlers—the Nevins family—set up camp in 1737.

The first household was set up by Deacon Thomas Nevins, who resettled from Bedford, Massachusetts. Married with two children, he built the first sound house in the area, which was then used for several years for town meetings.

Nevins's brother, William, moved in 1754 to Monson, where he raised five sons and three daughters. It's notable that all of his sons fought in the Revolutionary War.

Young Phineas, a lad of only sixteen or so, fell at the Battle of Bunker Hill. William Jr. was taken prisoner at the Battle of White Plains and died soon after.

"They sent him to a prison ship," Dickerman said. "When you were dead, they just tossed you overboard. Actually, I think they threw most of the prisoners overboard."

John disappeared somewhere in Charlestown, Massachusetts, and was never heard from again. Only Joseph and Benjamin survived the war.

The real trouble for Monson started with the outbreak of the French and Indian War in 1744. All of the small towns in central New Hampshire began to see themselves as being vulnerable to attack.

On May 13, 1747, the town petitioned the state: "Wherefore your petitioners that a guard for two garrisons and a small scout out front may be granted to us."

The garrisons were built, but there was no money to maintain them. It was just as well that there were no recorded raids by the local tribes.

Unfortunately, this petition was signed by only fourteen residents. And things got worse. In 1749, it was decided that the town should build a house of worship, as necessitated by the town charter. In 1753, however, Monson was so strapped for cash that townspeople petitioned the state to allow them to forego paying provincial taxes.

In 1758, a building site was proposed on the top of Federal Hill. It's known that they built something up there, but it doesn't seem to have done the trick, as a proposition was introduced in 1764 to appropriate funds "in order to make satisfaction to the town of Amherst and Hollis the privilege of worshipping with them."

Three years after that, the town voted that no money should be collected from the populace for this purpose. To add insult to injury, a proposal was introduced in 1760 that land on the south side of Monson should be annexed to Hollis.

It was clear to everyone that the writing was on the wall.

In 1770, the hardscrabble settlers finally gave up the ghost. They petitioned the general court to disassociate the town and repeal their charter, stating

> *that Land in and about the Center of Monson is so very poor, Broken, Baron and uneaven, as cannot admit of many Settlers, so that those Families that are in Town, are almost planted on the Extreme parts of it. We have no prospect of ever Building a Meeting-House in the Center or elsewhere, any ways to accommodate us, by which Difficulties we think the Gospel will not be settled among us while in the present situation. We therefore pray, etc.*

No other petition of this kind exists in New Hampshire.

The town was divided between Hollis and Milford; people moved out, and Monson Center was slowly abandoned.

And that was pretty much it. For the next 228 years, Monson Center remained a quiet anachronism of old roads and cellar holes, with the forest slowly swallowing it up.

Then, in 1998, everything changed, as the specter of imminent development raised its head. Some speculators thought the old town would be a great place to build twenty-eight luxury town houses. Immediately, Russ and Geri Dickerman leaped into the fray and began organizing an effort to save the old colonial town.

The Dickermans completely refurbished one of the homes on the site known as the Gault House. With an appointment, you can see a good representation of what a home was like in those days, complete with original furniture and portraits of some of the old residents. Trails are now marked with signs pointing out the cellar holes and who once occupied these homes.

The "Save Monson Center" movement was an enormous success. Russ and Geri Dickerman initially donated 125 acres to the effort, with the

The Monson animal pound, constructed in 1740 and restored by Russ Dickerman. *Photograph by the author.*

Society for the Protection of New Hampshire Forests stepping in and buying another 200 acres. There are now nearly 400 acres on the reservation, and it's still growing.

Monson is a particularly quiet and peaceful place. Of course, there are those who have visited it at night and will insist that they can still hear the turn of cartwheels, the sound of wood being cut and the quiet whisper of ancient conversation. It would appear that the citizens of this ancient township are still in residence, shades of some of the earliest settlers in this part of New Hampshire.

Obviously, even as Hillsborough County was established, there were already old legends in this area, and the spirits of the long dead were already occupying the land.

2
THE HAUNTED TOWN OF WILTON

As far as haunted towns go, Wilton is a relatively nondescript place—a small downtown, a couple of mills, a cluster of modest houses gathered about the banks of the Souhegan River. As for its history, however—well, let's just say that appearances aren't everything.

Wilton is a very weird town. For a start, there is Wilton Center, which isn't really in the center of Wilton at all but rides up aside the old Isaac Frye Highway. Secondly, it appears that the entire town is hunkered over a huge deposit of quartz, which, as anyone associated with spiritualism will tell you, is a very strong psychic medium.

If that weren't enough, Wilton's history is rife with odd and horrible events, many of which would readily provide a fertile bed for many varieties of paranormal phenomena.

When European settlers moved here in the early eighteenth century, these were the favored hunting grounds of a number of Native American tribes. The Pawtucket tribe, which was headquartered in what is now Lowell, Massachusetts, was prevalent in the area, as were the Pennacooks, hailing from present-day Manchester, New Hampshire. Then there were the Souhegans, who took their name from this low, shallow waterway, naming it "river of the plains."

The founding of the town is marked by tragedy. There is, for instance, the story of a massacre, as recounted by the ghost of a Native American warrior by the name of Sochemn, who was channeled by a local group of ghost hunters.

According to the North Eastern Paranormal Research Society (www.neprs.com), in his testimony, the spirit said three hundred of his people had traveled south to Wilton to celebrate the wedding of one of their own to a local chieftain's daughter. The white settlers, who had built their homes along the river, didn't take kindly to the arrival of the natives and brought them gifts with the intention of getting them to move along.

This didn't really take, however, and the Indians simply thought the whites were being hospitable. They intended to spend the winter there and move up back north in the spring.

According to Sochemn, things reached a head in the summer of 1744. It's interesting to note that the residents of Wilton had previously felt so secure in their habitation that they didn't even take the customary precaution of requesting a garrison for their protection. In that year, however, the people suddenly petitioned the British government to send them reinforcements against the Indians.

The petition read as follows: "We would pray your Excellency that we may have some assistance from the Government, in sending us some souldiers [*sic*] to Guard and Defend us as in your wisdom you shall think proper."

Vale End Cemetery, Wilton. *Photograph by the author.*

According to the spirit, the troops were sent in, and the tribe was massacred down to the last woman and child. Whether there is any truth to this story is up for speculation; there is, apparently, no record of a massacre in Wilton—but then, that wouldn't be surprising given the nature of the event.

What makes this story all the more interesting is the appearance of another entity at Vale End, which isn't actually a ghost but more of a demon, both revered and feared by Native Americans.

The creature in question is a Pukwudgie, a sort of three-foot-tall troll, straight out of the folklore of the Wampanoag Nation, the dominant Native American tribe in Massachusetts and southern New England, according to an article by Christopher Balzano at www.masscrossroads.com. There have been numerous sightings of these creatures in the cemetery, often chasing hapless explorers to the gates of the burying ground. According to folklore, it has the ability to appear and disappear at will and is fond of luring mortals to their doom over the edge of cliffs.

One might suppose the trolls' appearance is the result of the Native American curse on the white settlers in response to the alleged massacre. After all, that might explain some of the misfortunes that were visited on the community in ensuing years.

Tragedy at the Town Hall

In 1773, the residents of Wilton determined they were in need of a new meetinghouse. In April of that year, the town voted to provide six barrels of rum, a barrel of brown sugar, half a box of lemons and two loaves of sugar in order to fortify the men who would be raising the building.

On September 7, people gathered from miles around, eager for what was to be a day of celebration. Then, things went horribly wrong.

In the midst of construction, the huge central beam broke loose, and fifty-three men fell thirty feet to the ground, followed by tons of beams and building materials. Five of the men were killed outright, and many others were permanently crippled.

For a full account of the tragedy, we turn to the *New Hampshire Gazette*, from Portsmouth, which published the following report on September 24, 1773:

> *Last Tuesday the most melancholy Accident, of the kind, happened at Wilton, in New-Hampshire Government, that perhaps has been*

The Meeting House in Wilton Center. *Photograph by the author.*

known in the County—A Large Company was collected there to raise a Meeting House, and they got up the Body of it, the Beams and Joints, and these had laid a large quantity of Boards for the more convenient standing; they had also raised part of the Roof, in doing which they had occasion for a number of Crow-bars and Axes, which rested on the Building while the People got together, and were in the act of raising another double pair of Principles with a King-Post, when on a sudden the Beam under them broke at the Mortise in the middle, by which upwards of fifty Persons fell to the Bottom of the House with the Timber, Bars, Axes & ct. and exhibited a Scene to the astonish'd Spectators around the House (for there were no Persons in the Bottom of it, all having withdrawn thro' fear of what might happen) which can't be described; and could only be equaled by the Blood and Brains, Shrieks and Groans of the dead and wounded, which were immediately seen and heard—Three were killed outright, another survived but for a short time, and several others have since died of their Wounds' of fifty

> *three that fell not on escaped without broken Bones, terrible Bruises, or Wounds from the Axes &c. And as they were men pick'd from that and the neighboring Towns, and many of them heads of Families, the News of their Catastrophe filled those Places with Weeping, Lamentation and Woe, and may fully remind us all that "Man knoweth not his Time," but "as such an hour as we think not the Son of Man cometh," and it therefore concerns us to be always ready.*

THE BLUE LADY

Given this weird history, it's little wonder that the town has more than its fair share of specters. Probably the most famous of these is that of the Blue Lady, which is said to haunt Vale End Cemetery.

The ghost in question is that of Mary Ritter Spaulding, who was born on January 12, 1773. In 1795, she married Isaac Spaulding, a local tanner who could trace his lineage back to the original Jamestown settlers, and bore him seven children before her death on April 27, 1808, at only thirty-five years old. According to local legend, the Spauldings maintained a household on nearby Abbott Hill. It was there that Mary allegedly hanged herself after discovering that her husband had a mistress—who, incidentally, was also named Mary.

It is said that Mary was a kind and gentle woman, and this characterization has carried on in the years since her demise. In that time, there have been countless accounts of her ghost, known locally as the Blue Lady, walking the cemetery and the streets she knew in life. In response, many have left flowers and candles about her grave. Far from being an object of fear, she is seen as a benevolent spirit.

According to Hollow Hill, www.hollowhill.com, a website about ghosts by Fiona Broome, Mary is interred with Spaulding's second wife, Mary Flynn Colburn, which could account for some of her unrest. Hollow Hill describes Mary Ritter Spaulding as follows: "According to folklore, Mary Ritter Spaulding was a good, church-going woman who healed with herbs and prayer."

The official records show that Mary Spaulding's last child was Lyman, born in 1806. Paranormal investigators recently working at the site, however, maintain that they achieved contact with her spirit, and she was said to be troubled by the loss of her last child, James, born a year later.

Mary Ritter Spaulding's grave in Vale End Cemetery, Wilton. *Photograph by the author.*

There is no official proof of the birth of this child; he appears to have been lost in the mists of time.

Mary's gravestone sits almost at the edge of the woods, in a desolate corner of the cemetery. The top of the stone has been chipped away over the years and is now tipped with a jagged, irregular spike.

A few years ago, author Robin Ross Schoen purchased a brick Colonial on Sand Hill Road, which stands immediately adjacent to the cemetery. That's when she discovered her new ghostly neighbor.

"When I moved here, all of the local residents were very friendly," said Schoen. "They would invite me over for drinks or dinner, and they would all talk about the Blue Lady. Well, I began to get a little scared, and decided that I would go up to the place where she was buried and talk with her. Basically, I said that she had no idea what it took for me to get this house, and as I was here, we would just have to get along."

Although Schoen herself admits to never having seen the specter, her son did and promptly decided he'd be much more comfortable at a local hotel. Her granddaughter, Alex, also observed the ghost but had a much different reaction. She became enamored of the spirit and began to strike up a dialogue.

All of these events prompted Schoen to write a book about the situation entitled *Grandmother's Guest: The Blue Lady of Wilton*. It was, Schoen said, a project of significant duration, taking a full eight years of preparation.

"When I first started the book, I had such a hard time because I was trying to tell the story from my own viewpoint," Schoen said. "That's when I realized that I was going at it all wrong. I should have been telling it from my granddaughter's point of view. After all, children connect better with certain things than we do."

For Schoen, the situation became even stranger when she purchased a small pitcher at auction for her granddaughter.

"It's a little Staffordshire pitcher, with the handle broken and then repaired with staples," she said. "Inside, we found a note, simply inscribed 'Mary Ritter Spaulding,' with the date 1850. Alex came to the conclusion that this belonged to our Mary, but the date was all wrong—it was much too late. Eventually, after doing some research, I discovered that Mary had a granddaughter with the exact same name who would have been eight years old at that time. So the whole thing dovetailed together in a very intriguing way."

For the illustrations, Schoen enlisted noted artist Gail Hoar, who was more than happy to help. With each page involving a complete oil painting, it was an arduous and time-consuming task.

"The reason why I decided to illustrate it was because it was a New England story but with universal appeal," Hoar said. "It's the kind of tale you would want to pass on to your children and grandchildren. There's something very warm and appealing about it."

Despite all of these positive signs, Schoen still had some reservations about writing a children's book involving the supernatural. Eventually, however, she found those fears were groundless.

"Children weren't scared at all," she said. "Mary was such a gentle soul that they can sense that. As a matter of fact, I went up to the graveyard one day and visited her resting place. The epitaph pretty much says it all: 'Her serenity of temper and gentleness of manner threw a charm over a brief and peaceful life.' I thought that was just lovely."

Another psychic hot spot is about a half mile from the Vale End Cemetery: the Langdell House, where Mary Ritter was supposed to have spent her childhood. Closed since the 1930s, the house has an evil reputation. One of the tenants allegedly died in the attic, and after that, "figures" were regularly seen standing in the windows.

A local paranormal investigator, intrigued by the tales, decided to make an examination of the attic. Unfortunately, he fell through the rotting floorboards, went straight through the second floor and through the kitchen floor and died in the cellar. There, it's alleged, he joined the other spirits

The Langdell House in Wilton. Abandoned since the 1930s, it is alleged to be the childhood home of Mary Ritter Spaulding. *Photograph by the author.*

haunting the house. Whether any of these claims are true is moot, as the house is now locked up tighter than a drum.

"I actually visited the house at one point," Schoen admitted. "It was really strange—the furniture was still there, and there were books just sitting on the shelves. It was as if the residents just cleared out overnight."

The Town Hall

Disaster visited Wilton again on the morning of December 2, 1874, as a devastating fire wiped out virtually all of the downtown business district. The *New York Herald* described the event in its December 3 edition:

> *MILFORD, Dec. 2. All the business part of Wilton was destroyed this morning. The fire was discovered at Wallace's block, at five o'clock. The only fire engine in the place was frozen up and useless. The street was narrow and the flames quickly caught the Whiting House, a large hotel, kept by Dr. W. Jones, and burned it to the ground. The stores of Frank Kent, confectionary; D.B. Needham, dry goods; W.J. Bradbury, druggist; George Wallace, clothing store; Dr. Trevette, druggist, and N.D. Foster, stoves, were destroyed. Whiting's stable was burned, but the horses and carriages were saved. W.E. Jaques dry goods, Smith's barber shop and Taggart's boot and shoe, under the Whiting House, were burnt out. The residence of Mr. Barrett was the only dwelling house burned. The savings bank preserved all its books, but the interior of the building was burnt out. The fire company from Milford was sent for and reached Wilton at eight o'clock. Through their efforts Baldwin's block was saved and the fire checked. A steamer from Nashua arrived at a later hour and assisted in putting out the fire.*
>
> *The village was a flourishing one on the Boston Lowell and Greenfield road, but has suffered severely recently. A flood swept away one of its mills; a fire destroyed another, and a recent defalcation had borne heavily on its business men. The loss of all the best business houses now nearly cripples the place—only four stores remaining. Some of the losers show commendable pluck. While the fire still raged D.B. Needham engaged a room for his goods, and will resume business. The first express out bore an order for new Post Office boxes from W.S. Bradbury, postmaster. He will again open his store, though on a smaller scale. Cinders from the conflagration reached Milford, five miles away.*

Two more fires occurred over the next eleven years, the last on December 4, 1885. Once again, the residents rebuilt the downtown and constructed a new town hall, in 1886, on the site of the Whiting Hotel. Over the intervening years, this structure has served as a municipal center, a police station and a jail. In the early years of the twentieth century, it also acted as a theater, hosting traveling shows and vaudeville troupes. In 1912, the facility was converted into a silent movie house. Its popularity grew over the years; during World War II, it was the only place where locals could see newsreels. The cinema remains open to this day and now shows a variety of offbeat art films.

It is also extremely haunted.

Owner Dennis Markaverich has had a unique opportunity to witness these spirits firsthand, as he cleans the theater each night in preparation for the next day's showings. According to Markaverich, one of the most prominent ghosts in the place is that of a young boy named Henry that haunts the landing of the staircase leading to the second floor. He believes the specter is that of a boy whose parents died in the fire that he himself set.

The town hall on Main Street, Wilton. *Photograph by the author.*

That's not all. There also is a tall man adorned with a black stovepipe hat who is often seen walking down the center aisle of the theater. Additionally, there is another ghost in the ladies' restroom that often can be seen in the mirror.

For a town as small as Wilton, it has more than its share of ghosts. Sometimes, it seems, the paranormal can appear where you least expect it.

3

The Traveling Haunt

Do ghosts attach themselves to objects and follow them, even when they move? Certainly that seems to be the opinion of the members of the Rindge Historical Society, which presently operates out of the Freeborn Stearns House in that town; as soon as it began bringing in historical mementos from all over the state, including several guns from the Civil War, it started experiencing a gamut of paranormal activity.

The same could be said for a situation where an entire house moves, as is the case with the old Deacon Cummings House, presently located in Davis Court in the Historical District of Nashua. The house, a classic saltbox building, was originally constructed in Dunstable in 1746. In about 1800, the town border was moved, and the house was now located in what was now part of Hollis, specifically on Merrill Lane near Runnell's Bridge. The Runnel family ran a large farm and hired numerous itinerant workers to work on the property.

It is here that the legend of the house originates. It is said that one of the employees was an old sailor who harbored a severe distrust of banks and preferred to hide the jewels and loot he had acquired on his journeys under his pillow, along with a knife kept there for protection.

Well, the knife didn't do him any good. The other workers quickly learned of his cache and murdered him in his bed. After that point, it is said, his spirit began to stalk the house.

The house stood deserted for many years, and its reputation as a haunted place began to become pervasive. In 1896, the house came to the attention

Runnells Bridge in Hollis. *Nineteenth-century postcard.*

of one William Spalding, who heard of the place while at a party held at the Nashua Boat Club. He went into the vacant building to investigate three flashes of light the color of phosphorous. When he and his friends entered the house with candles, a gust of wind extinguished them, and bricks fell from the steeply pitched roof to the ground. Spalding purchased the house that year and moved it to its present location behind his Concord Street house.

Just what kind of person was Spalding—and what could have compelled him to purchase and move a demonstrably haunted house? We can glean some history of his family from *The Granite Monthly: A New Hampshire Magazine Devoted to History, Biography, Literature and State Progress*, edited by Henry Harrison Metcalf and John Norris McClintock and published in 1902:

> *The banking institutions of the city are not only large in number for a community of its size, but are noted in the financial world for successful management and strength of resources. The First National bank, located opposite the city hall, has occupied its own building for thirty-five years. Its president is the Hon. J.A. Spalding, present postmaster of Nashua; and a man known throughout the state for his long identification with its business, financial, political and other interests. Mr. Spalding was the first cashier of*

> *the First National, serving for the long period of thirty-two years. He is a native of Wilton and yet retains in his possession the homestead and estate. On his election as president of the bank, his son, William E. Spalding, was chosen his successor as cashier. He is one of the best known of the younger men in the city, for he has always been active and prominent in all that concerned its welfare. He was a member of the staff of Governor Rollins, and since then has carried the title of "general" and as General Spalding he is known about the state, but to his intimates and boyhood friends he is still familiarly designated as "Will."*
>
> *General Spalding has a hobby, and a splendid success he has made of it. It is the collection of all that in any manner pertained to home life in the Colonial times, and his effort along this line is so complete as to include the acquisition of a Colonial house of the better type, and the filling of it with the furniture, plate, dishes, and in fact, practically every article used by the pioneers of state and nation. The house stands on the spacious lawn of General Spalding's Concord street residence, and it and its contents constitute a collection at once so complete, great and varied that it could not fail to elicit the admiration and even astonishment of an Alice Morse Earle and other students of Colonial days.*

There were some alterations made to the property when Spalding purchased it; elements of the Colonial Revival were added, including a corner cupboard with fluted columns and a detailed cornice. Most of the building, however, remained intact.

It's interesting to note that Concord Street had its own history of ghosts long before Spalding brought "the Haunt" into the neighborhood. For instance, we have the following account from the *Portland Daily Press*, published on July 12, 1871:

> *HAUNTED HOUSE IN NASHUA—The State House at Concord has for several weeks been haunted by a lively set of political ghosts from all parts of the State, nevertheless Nashua presents a case of which the following statement is made:*
>
> *Some three years ago a well-known gentleman purchased a house on the Concord road. He had not long resided in his peaceful villa when of a moonlight night, he was aroused by what seemed to be a flock of sheep walking on the roof above his head. Of course he was puzzled to understand the phenomenon; more so when he sought to learn the cause and discovered—nothing. Since that time persons have been heard in*

> *conversation in the cellar, and the sound of someone digging in the earth under the windows with crowbars. Occasionally there has been an offensive effluvia ascend from the hearth in one of the rooms, and the family have been subjected to a variety of other annoyances.*
>
> *On Friday night last week the gentleman heard what* [he] *supposed to be some splitting of wood in the shed, and descending quietly to an adjoining door with a lighted lamp, listened to the sound for a full hour; in the meantime hearing noises in the kitchen at his left which led him to suppose that some other member of the family was about, he opened the door, and as usual, there was nothing in either place. These noises have become so frequent and have been so often repeated that the wife's and sons' health have suffered, and the gentleman has been obliged to make arrangements for their accommodation elsewhere. He now proposes to invite a few friends to join him in a full investigation of this mysterious affair. The result will be made available at an early day.*

That's not all. There was another haunted encounter in the same neighborhood about ten years later. This one was particularly heinous, as we find in a report from the *Boston Journal* on November 16, 1880:

> *Nashua has a "haunted house." It is situated within the half mile radius of the geographical center of the city. It is a large, two-story modern and tenantless structure. It has been built five or six years, and from its portal mother and son have passed to the grave. Just now this house is the sensation of the city. Everybody is talking about it and the wonderful phenomena that have occurred within its four walls are the evening themes of many family circles. Those who are superstitious have an idea that the spirits of the departed linger here, for what purpose is not clear, and those who are of a practical turn of mind laugh in derision, and while they do not ignore the statement that strange and thus far unaccountable sounds have been heard, they urge that an intelligent investigation will reveal natural causes. We express no opinion, we simply give numerous statements, many of which we have from the lips of those who learned them by experience.*
>
> *A family took possession of the house. The first evening, while the wife, with her children about her, was engaged about some work in the parlor, the door bell rang. She answered the summons, and to her great surprise, there was no one at the door. She returned to her work and presently she heard footsteps in the hall. She sought to learn the individuality of her visitor and was dismayed upon discovering—nobody. During the night*

that followed strange, unexplainable noises were heard, and the members of the family began to fear they had become tenants of a haunted house. The next night there was a general racket. At midnight the household was aroused by a sound which indicated that the covers of the stove were being shuffled about and someone was engaged in housework. The head of the family and a male lodger—a partially deaf man who was aroused by the noise—investigated in the kitchen and no cause could be found. They retired, when presently a stove in the attic of the house was thumped and banged about. No cause could be discovered. During the next few nights a noise like a person strangling with hiccough, also groanings and traveling about the halls and upon the stairs were heard and no clue to a cause could be assigned. It is also said that the store covers were rattled during the day, and when the wife, thinking some friend had called and was making the noise to attract her attention, opened the door, there was a pressure against her like a person crowding past, also that she was crowded in a like manner while ascending the staircase. The family moved out.

Since then there has been an endless amount of speculation, and all the ghost stories of individual recollection have been told and retold to the wonderment and entertainment of select circles. The troubles of this haunted house have also been continued, and stories about it have magnified until the most wonderful phenomena of the age are attributed to it.

A gentleman who proposed to hire it undertook, with a friend, to spend the night in it, but the traveling about the hall, ringing of the doorbell, rapping upon the walls, and a bright light which was frequently thrown into their faces from "nowhere in particular," frightened them so that they fled at midnight in dismay.

Mediums have held séances in the house and profess to have held solemn conversations with those who died there, and it is told that on a certain night a bright light was seen for an hour in the room, where the woman, mentioned in the first paragraph, died.

We dislike to spoil a good story, but since the foregoing was written, a gentleman residing in the neighborhood of the haunted house has informed The Telegraph *that the strange phenomena are traceable to a family of rats that had made a nest in the furnace.*

In its new location, the house attracted the attention of the press at large. As it predated just about every other building in the city, it was seen as something of an oddity. As an example, we have this rather curious little piece from the June 30, 1904 edition of the *Weekly Advocate*:

AN ODD OLD HOUSE
Quaint New Hampshire Building That Dates Back 250 Years.
Col. William E. Spalding, known throughout New England as a collector of antiques and owning some of the best specimens of Colonial utilities to be found in any one collection, some seven or eight year ago secured from the Nashua Hollis line the Winslow Reed house, a curious old structure more than 250 years old, which was first brought to general notice by the Press, *which published some interesting ghost stories based on peculiar happenings at the isolated farmhouse. This house was taken down and transported piecemeal to Col. Spalding's lawns, where it was rebuilt and filed with the choicest and most appropriate antiques to be bought at any price in New England. Today it stands a priceless storehouse of treasures.*

In the old house are secret cupboards and strange, weird closets. Most strange of all is a secret stairway winding around the immense chimney, which leads to a secret chamber on the second floor, large enough for ten or twelve persons and yet so arranged as to be without chance of discovery to the rest of the house. In the cellar was a room in the chimney where it is believed counterfeiting was going on.

It appears that the house was in imminent danger of demolition at the beginning of the twentieth century. For instance, we have this account from the December 27, 1906 edition of the *Boston Herald*:

The "Haunt," the historic dwelling house moved to this city by Gen. William E. Spalding, where it was the old building (10 years ago), and fitted up as a special building in which Gen. Spalding kept his famous collection of antique furniture and historical relics, is being dismantled.

Gen. Spalding this week disposed of all of his collection except that which he has moved into his residence on Abbott Square, and the sale was one of the most notable events of the kind which has taken place in New England for years. There were dealers and collectors present from all parts of New England. Extraordinarily high prices prevailed.

This was especially true in the matter of highboys, lowboys, sofas, chairs and other articles of high class old-fashioned furniture, and on Sheffield silver and pewter ware.

Extensive purchases were made by Hollis French, Dwigin Kinney and Mrs. Lord of Boston. Mrs. Caarks Curis of Manchester, Mrs. Harry Putnam of Concord, Mrs. Heddrick of Lowell, Dr. George F. Newcombe of Somersworth, Dr. Charles Twitchell of Portland, Me., and Mrs.

Barrows of Haverhill while Mr. Merritt of Lowell, a well known book collector, purchased a large stock in his line.

The "Haunt" was originally constructed in Dunstable, Mass., in 1746, but its builder or first owner is not known. About 1800 it was moved across the town line into Hollis, and was the first wood frame building in which a resident of that town was known to have lived. A diary possessed by George A. Burke of Hollis tells of the removal of the building into the town being drawn by oxen.

It was located in the vicinity of Runnell's Falls on the Nashua River on the highway between this city and Pepperell Mass., and as long ago as the memory of the oldest inhabitant dates back it had the reputation of being a "haunted" house. For years it was deserted.

Gen. Spalding upon purchasing it, moved it to a location in the rear of his former residence on Concord Street in this city, and restored it at considerable expense, although he found at that time that the timbers were in a fine state of preservation.

It formed a fitting place to display to his friends his collection of antiques to which he was constantly adding, and which came to be known as one of the best in New England. His decision to break it up came as a surprise to dealers and collectors all over this part of the country.

An effort is being made on the Matthew Thornton chapter D.A.R. of this city to purchase the building, fix it up as a meeting place, and keep in it such historical articles as the society may be able to procure.

Gen. Spalding was one of the New Hampshire agents at the time of the St. Louis exposition, and from his collection a number of articles were taken to furnish a room in the New Hampshire building on the exposition grounds.

From these accounts, it would appear that General Spalding was liquidating his treasured collection in order to decamp to other environs. The Daughters of the American Revolution was evidently successful in its attempts to secure the ancient structure, and it stands today, converted back into a private dwelling.

General Spalding lived a good sixteen years longer, expiring in 1922. From the May 24 edition of the *Boston Herald* of that year, we have his funeral notice:

The funeral of William E. Spalding, Boston financier, will be held this afternoon at Nashua, N.H., where he resided before coming to Boston. He died Monday, following an operation. He is believed to have owned the

> *finest antique collection in this part of the country. He leaves a widow, Florence Dexter Spalding, a son and a daughter.*
>
> *He was the owner of the famous King Hooper mansion in Marblehead and the Spalding farm house, which is in Parker street back of the Wentworth Institute in Roxbury. He served on the staffs of Gov. Sawyer and Gov. Rollins in New Hampshire. He was always interested in amateur entertaining and was prominent in the Longwood Minstrels and in the shows which the 1st corps Cadets gave in former years. He was a member of the Boston Athletic Association.*

It's a little fuzzy what happened to the house after 1906, but it seems to have been converted back into a private home. What I have been able to determine is that an architect by the name of Steven Tracy purchased the house in 1942 and used it as an office. Consequently, he kept it heated and moisture free, which accounts for its continued good condition. He also preserved the wall panels and the hand-hewn thirty-inch boards. The captain's staircase to the second floor was preserved, as was the "good morning" staircase to the attic. In 1968, the house was sold to Nashua alderman Linda Willett, who lived there with her husband, Henry, and their three children.

The house still stands in Davis Court, hidden behind an ornate garden. From the street, it still looks imposing and is definitely one of Nashua's true architectural treasures. Few people, however, seem to be aware of its incredibly haunted history.

4

The Spirits of Gilson Cemetery

Over the many years that I've been writing ghost stories, I've always been struck by the preconceptions that surround the sites themselves. I mean, I do a fair amount of research on the Internet, as well as discussing the place with representatives of various paranormal societies.

Whether this is a good idea, I'm not sure. Certainly, this practice can color your perception, and not always in a good way. On the other hand, it can give you an idea of what to look for.

This particular expedition took me out to the Gilson Road Cemetery, a tiny plot of land right across the road from the Tanglewood housing estate. For the uninitiated, Gilson Road Cemetery has a considerable reputation in paranormal investigation circles. The ghosts that inhabit this little plot of land were first observed over a decade ago by Fiona Broome, a famous investigator who runs the Hollow Hills website. Since that time, the site has become a favored gathering point for ghost hunters from all over the country. I thought I'd take a trip out there to see what all the fuss was about.

This is not an easy place to find. I took the exit onto Route 111 and thought myself totally lost. Spotting a man fixing the front of his garage, I decided to pull over and ask directions.

"There's a gas station a little ways down the road," the man helpfully informed me. "Take a right there. That's Gilson Road. Of course, it kind of winds around a bit."

It certainly did. For a while there, I wondered if I was on the right road. When I finally came upon the cemetery itself, I almost drove completely past the place. I actually had to back up when I caught sight of an ancient stone wall.

The cemetery is significantly smaller than one would expect. I doubt it even covers an acre of land. There are a few stones here and there and lots of impressions in the ground that designate where other, older graves probably stood. The oldest stone I saw here was that of Hannah, wife of Benjamin Robbins, who died on January 29, 1796, at the tender age of twenty years. The other families interred here include the Gilsons, the Fisks, the Searles, Lawrences and Newtons.

In the front of the cemetery stands the burial spot of the Gilson family. John Gilson died on March 17, 1837. His wife, Betsey, followed him into the Great Beyond some three years later. Between their graves are three small headstones, simply stating that they bear memorial to their unnamed babies, who died in infancy. I was rather touched by the fact that visitors had placed small toys and Halloween candies on their graves.

Easily the strangest stone in the entire cemetery belongs to young Walter Gilson, son of Joseph and Lucy, who died on August 28, 1811, aged five

Gilson Road Cemetery, photographed on a quiet fall afternoon. *Photograph by the author.*

The graves of the three unnamed Gilson babies, adorned with toys and candy. *Photograph by the author.*

years, eight months and twenty-five days. The odd thing about this stone is a hole, about an inch in diameter, drilled directly into the center of the stone. Clearly, it is not the result of a gunshot, as there are no radiating cracks from around the center of the incision. Rather, it is a completely clean radial hole, as if someone had taken a drill to it. At this point, I have absolutely no idea what purpose the hole could have ever had.

History records that there was a John Gilson who was actually one of the first people to settle in what is now Nashua. Given the timeline, one can only assume that this was an ancestor of the man buried in the cemetery. For more information about this expedition, we turn to *The History of Nashua*, written by John H. Goodale and published in 1885:

> *A TRAMP THROUGH THE WILDERNESS—In the fall of 1747 two explorers from Dunstable, Nehemiah Lovewell and John Gilson, started from the present site of Nashua for the purpose of examining the slope of the Merrimack Valley and of crossing the height of land to*

Walter Gilson's grave. Note the strange hole drilled through the center of the stone. *Photograph by the author.*

Number Four (now Charlestown), which was then known as the most northern settlement in the Connecticut Valley. Knowing the difficulties in traversing hills and valleys covered with underbrush and rough with fallen timber and huge bowlders [sic], *they carried as light an outfit as possible—a musket and camp-blanket each, with five days' provisions. Following the Souhegan through Milford to Wilton, they then turned northward, and, crossing the height of land in the limits of the present day Stoddard, had, on the afternoon of the third day, their first view of the broad valley westward, with a dim outline of the mountains beyond. The weather was clear and pleasant, the journey laborious, but invigorating. On their fourth afternoon they reached and camped for the night on the banks of the Connecticut, some ten miles below Charlestown. At noon of the next day they were welcomed at the rude fort, which had already won renown by the heroic valor of its little garrison. At this time the forest was commanded by Captain Phineas Stevens, a man of great energy and bravery. Lovewell and Gilson were the first visitors from the valley of the Merrimack, and their arrival was a novelty. That night—as in later years, they used to relate—they sat up until midnight, listening to a recital of the fierce struggles which the inmates of this rude fortress, far up in the woods, had encountered within the previous eight months. Tarrying several days at the fort, during which the weather continued clear and mild, the two explorers were ready to return homeward. In a direct line Dunstable was about ninety miles distant. With the needed supply of salt pork and corn bread, Lovewell and Gilson left Number Four at sunrise on the 16th of November. The fallen leaves were crisp with frost as they entered the deep maple forests which skirt the hills lying east of the Connecticut intervales. The days being short, it was necessary to lose no time between sunrise and sunset. The air was cool and stimulated them to vigorously hurry forward.*

> *Coming to a clear spring soon after midday, Gilson struck a fire and resting for half an hour, they sat down to a marvelously good feast of boiled salt pork and brown bread. One who has never eaten a dinner under like conditions can have no idea of its keen relish and appreciation.*

The details of how the cemetery was founded are extremely vague, shrouded in local folklore. It is said by some that the spirits of the place are engendered by a fierce battle among the Native Americans that took place on the spot. According to these same legends, it is believed that the area was sacred to the Indians, and when the land was blessed, the spirits of their dead rose up and began to stalk the cemetery. Another legend maintains that it was to this area that an insane medicine man was banished, and he still haunts the place. It is said that, during his life, he would lure young braves here, promising to give them spirits that would aid them in battle. Instead, he would sacrifice the young men to his own dark spirits and use their energy to prolong his life. Then there is the story of the "Gilson Boy," who is seen running across the road and disappears the moment he is approached. Many years ago, it was reported, the site was allegedly used by a serial killer as the dumping ground for the bodies of young boys. There is also a tale involving a mother and her two children, who perished in a house fire here at some point.

Stories of ghosts here are legion. Many investigators report hearing strange whispers as they enter the cemetery, while others have seen strange lights emanating from the back wall. Photographs taken there show orbs, specters and other paranormal phenomena. There are also reports of a ghostly woman in a white dress that is frequently seen wandering the perimeter of the site.

Other reported ghosts include a black hooded figure frequently seen walking through the graveyard. Another commonly reported phenomenon is the sound of whispering, which seems to emanate throughout the site. Glittering lights have been seen in the surrounding woods, and large entities can be heard moving around the back perimeter.

The supernatural activities seem to have spread to some of the older houses surrounding the cemetery. There have been reports of glasses breaking, doors and windows opening and closing of their own accord and mysterious cold spots. Additionally, the sports field attached to the local elementary school has demonstrated paranormal phenomena, as voices have been heard and apparitions observed. Some investigators maintain that the field is protected by some kind of entity.

An ectoplasmic manifestation photographed at Gilson Road Cemetery. *SilentWhispers Paranormal Group.*

A strange mist surrounds one of the stones at Gilson Road Cemetery. *SilentWhispers Paranormal Group.*

"One of the first things you encounter upon entering the cemetery is a kind of green mist," said Theresa Harlow-Sillanpaa of the Conscious Spirit Paranormal Group. "It seems to move around the graves. When I investigated the cemetery, I encountered a spirit of a man in the vicinity of the three child graves situated between the stones of John and Mary Gilson. People have left toys on the stones, and those also seem to move around by themselves."

One of the more startling spirits haunting the cemetery is an entity known locally as "the biker." A number of paranormal investigators have reported encountering this spirit, a man clearly of the twentieth century. Harlow-Sillanpaa, however, has a particular trump card in this regard; she claims to have actually photographed the spirit.

"He's a dark-haired man wearing a leather jacket," she said. "He's leaning against one of the monuments, smoking a cigarette. You can completely see through him. There's also another spirit to the left of him, but that one is somewhat indistinct. You can't really make it out."

A strange orange manifestation photographed at Gilson Road Cemetery. *SilentWhispers Paranormal Group.*

Above: The gate at the Gilson Road Cemetery. Note the mist floating behind the large letter "G" and a small orb floating on the right. *SilentWhispers Paranormal Group.*

Right: The graves of the Gilson family in the Gilson Road Cemetery. *Photograph by the author.*

For more information about the spirits that stalk this cemetery, I turned to T.J. Swick, co-founder of the SilentWhispers Paranormal Society, who had some particularly creepy encounters at the spot.

"The very first time we went there was back in 2008," she said. "We were just driving around when we stumbled upon the cemetery. I didn't really know anything about the place at the time, but we noted that there weren't any signs telling us to stay out after dark. So we decided it would by OK to investigate. I started taking photographs and immediately got a red streak running over one of the stones."

Like many other investigators, Swick noted that the entire team began to experience a peculiar heaviness, as though walking through water.

"At one point, I was walking away from Walter Gilson's grave toward the gate," she said. "Angel, co-founder of the society, was walking ahead of me, along with another gentleman. Suddenly, I heard the sound of someone running up behind me. I turned around, but there was nobody behind me. Later on, however, I discovered various accounts alleging that the spirit of Walter Gilson had a habit of chasing people around."

It's interesting to note that though Walter's parents, Joseph and Lucy, are buried at the site, the grave of their son is a good distance from them. It's very strange that the grave should be by itself. And then there is also the fact of the mysterious hole drilled right through the center of the stone.

Further investigations led to some other bizarre encounters.

"We decided to bring some high school seniors with us for their first ghost hunt," Swick said. "We were taking some photographs and videos when my daughter felt somebody touch her inappropriately. One of the other seniors told the ghost to stop it when the voice recorder suddenly said, 'Bastard.' I was totally shocked."

And that's not all. Angel had a disturbing encounter with a strange hooded figure.

"It was standing outside the wall by the gate," Swick said. "The figure was completely black, with glowing red eyes. I photographed the area, but outside of a few orbs, I didn't get anything. Later on, I discovered that other people had encountered this same entity over the years."

When Swick's son came up from Florida for a visit, he requested a visit to the cemetery. Right on cue, odd visitations began to make themselves felt.

"My son was standing in front of the three child stones and read the words, 'Baby Gilson, Baby Gilson, Baby Gilson.' Almost immediately, a

A shot of the back wall of Gilson Road Cemetery. Note the face of a young woman (circled). *SilentWhispers Paranormal Group.*

woman's voice came through, saying very quickly something that sounded like 'cunamuninae.' It was very fast and very clear."

Although no such word exists in the English language, there is a word in a Caribbean dialect, *cunumunu*, meaning an idiot or simple person. Bearing in mind that a lot of the early settlers had Caribbean slaves, it is entirely possible that one of them was actually insulting the speaker.

So is this cemetery really haunted? It would appear, from the amount of interest it has excited among ghost hunters, that something is definitely going on there. Really, with a history like this, it would be exceedingly strange if there weren't any restless spirits roaming around. Beware, though—from everything I've heard, the spirits there are restless and not particularly inviting to interlopers.

5

FRANCESTOWN

HAUNTED POND AND THE GIBSON TAVERN

You'd never think there was anything strange or bizarre about the village of Francestown. As a matter of fact, it's almost a postcard-perfect image of the rural New England village. The center is lorded over by the pristine white meetinghouse with an ancient graveyard behind it and old stately houses gathered on each side, lined up like ancient matrons. The Francestown Village Store seems to be the only real business in town, selling sandwiches, coffee and takeout meals to the residents. Right next to the door, there is a pile of T-shirts for sale. "What happens in Francestown, stays in Francestown," they declare. "But nothing ever happens in Francestown."

The town was named after Frances Wentworth Deering, the wife of John Wentworth, governor of New Hampshire. In his youth, Wentworth was a man of means and ambition. Frances, his cousin, acted as a maid in his household. During his time as a student at Harvard, things got a little hot and heavy between the two, and Frances began to entertain ideas of marriage.

It was not to be. Upon graduation, John scooted to England, leaving a despondent Frances behind. Not to worry, though; one Theodore Atkinson Jr., another cousin, was all too eager to fill the breach and began his own wooing campaign. They were married on May 13, 1762. Frances was only sixteen years of age. They then moved to Portsmouth, where they expected to enjoy a long and happy marriage

Their bucolic days were numbered, however. Shortly after the wedding, Theodore came down with what was then known colloquially as a "lingering

Governor John Wentworth, painted in 1769 by John Singleton Copley. *Hood Museum of Art, Dartmouth College, Hanover, New Hampshire.*

illness." Meanwhile, John Wentworth had returned to New Hampshire, appointed as governor to the colony.

This is where things became decidedly peculiar. John Wentworth moved into a house right down the road from the beleaguered couple.

As Theodore's health declined, his wife began to entertain certain thoughts about her former suitor. Accordingly, she devised various ways to keep the governor abreast of the current state of her husband's health. One of these involved opening a window in the upper story of her house and waving a white piece of cloth where John could see it. This implied, in essence, that Theodore was still breathing.

Finally, on October 28, 1769, Theodore shuffled off this mortal coil. What happened next sent tongues wagging throughout New England. Theodore Atkinson was scarcely cold in his grave before Frances began plotting her next conquest. Harriet E.P. Spofford recounts the scandal in *New England Legends* (1871):

> *On one day Theodore breathed his last. His burial took place on the following Wednesday; by the Governor's order all the bells in town were tolled, flags were hung at half-mast, and minute-guns were fired from the fort and from the ships-of-war in the harbor. On Sunday the weeping widow, clad in crapes, listened in church to the funeral eulogies; on Monday her affliction was mitigated; on Tuesday all the fingers of all the seamstresses of the country roundabout were flying; and on the next Sunday, in the white satins and jewels and fardingales of a bride, she walked up the aisle, the wife of Governor Wentworth.*

In the year 1772, Wentworth decided to name a newly incorporated village after his bride, and Francestown was born. Incidentally, he accorded the same honor to another town two years later, when the town of Deering came into fruition.

Frances Deering Atkinson signaling to Governor Wentworth that her husband was still alive. *From* New England Legends, *by Harriet E.P. Spofford, 1871.*

Powerful as he was, things didn't go so well for John Wentworth when hostilities with Britain broke out later that decade. As an avowed Tory, he soon found that a considerable portion of the populace harbored a deep animosity toward him. Consequently, the couple was forced to flee New Hampshire. As it turned out, however, things weren't really that bad; for his loyalty to the Crown, Wentworth was awarded the governorship of Nova Scotia, and Frances was appointed a lady-in-waiting at the English court.

Francestown, meanwhile, continued on its sleepy way, being a collection of farms and pastures. Then, in 1794, one Daniel Fuller discovered soapstone in his field while plowing.

Well, that changed everything. By the early nineteenth century, three quarries were operating in full vigor in the town, and Francestown was widely acknowledged as the producer of some of the finest soapstone in the country. The stone was in considerable demand. New England colonists used it for stove backs, inkstands, bed warmers, tombstones and griddles. It was also indispensable in the construction of some of the earliest free-standing woodstoves. Eventually, however, the demand for the stone petered out somewhat, and Fuller's quarry closed in 1891. The village subsequently went back to its agrarian roots.

A couple years back, I was working as a reporter at the local newspaper, the *Monadnock Ledger-Transcript*. I had several regular beats in the area, Francestown among them. One day, I was assigned to cover the construction of a new bridge, which was to replace one destroyed by flood a few years earlier. Not being familiar with the village, however, I was obliged to visit the town offices in order to ascertain just where I was going.

As I was standing in the office, looking over a map of the town, a certain aspect of the area immediately caught my eye. There was a small body of water labeled "Haunted Lake." Being of an inquisitive frame of mind, I inquired of the secretary about this particular location.

"You really don't want to know about that," came the terse reply.

Well, in my case, that's a bit like waving a red flag in front of a bull. I immediately made a mental note to check this place out as soon as possible.

A couple weeks later, I made the trip out to the lake. It wasn't easy; the roads leading out there are largely just dirt trails, and my car was definitely not happy with the terrain. Nonetheless, I did eventually find the place, pulled over and began my trek into the forest.

I have to admit, I was scared. It wasn't so much about the prospect of meeting ghosts that unnerved me, however, as traversing the amount of deadfall that I encountered in these woods. I was certain that I would sustain some kind of leg injury as I staggered over fallen logs and wet leaves. As I finally made my way to the edge of the lake itself, I discovered a place that more than lived up to its ominous reputation. A light mist had settled on the water, which was as smooth as a pane of glass. The trees on the far side of the water were shrouded in a thick mantle of fog, and the place was deathly silent. Far off, the mournful hoot of a loon echoed through the morning air, lending a final macabre touch to the scene.

As lakes go, this one isn't particularly large. It also appears to be quite shallow. It is remarkable, therefore, that this body of water has such a nasty reputation, as a number of people have met their premature deaths in its waters.

The first was a twelve-year-old boy named Jacob Langdell, who was drowned on July 11, 1813. When the body was discovered, a bunch of lilies were found to be clasped in his hand. Over the years, more bodies were dredged from the lake. A boy by the name of Samuel Allen perished in its waters in 1816; Ichabod Gay followed him to a watery grave on June 20, 1824; and one Nathaniel Aiken shared his fate in 1830.

A view of Haunted Pond in Francestown. *Photograph by the author.*

The history of how the lake got its sobriquet is a little clouded, and several tales have come up that would account for it. Apparently, it has always been known as "Haunted Pond" or "Haunted Lake" right back to when the village was originally founded. One explanation is that there was once a fire that raged on its shores that was so fierce that everything along the perimeter was consumed. All that was left was a black, twisted mess of branches and trees, the skeletal remains of the forest that once thrived there. It left such an impression on the early surveyors that they attributed supernatural ramifications to the area.

The lake is fed by a number of small streams, among them Whiting Brook. For an in-depth explanation of the topography of the area, we turn to *The History of Francestown, N.H. from Its Earliest Settlement April 1758 to 1891*, by Warren Robert Coltrain and George K. Wood:

> *Whiting Brook, which empties into Scoby Pond, or "Haunted Lake," on the north, rises near Weare line, is about three miles long, flows nearly south, has at one place a broken fall, somewhat remarkable, of 15 feet, has broad pools of clear water, like the White Mountain streams, and, after having crossed the New Boston road and received the Pettee Brook, it really becomes quite a pretentious stream, cutting a wide channel through the meadows. For a quarter of a mile before entering the Lake, it is deep, dark, sluggish, over-hung with banks, and resembles a small Florida creek, alligators and cypress excepted. And for this distance the fisherman rows his boat up the stream, and counts it a favorite place to drop the line. There are no mills on this stream, and it has been noted for suckers in spring and trout in summer.*

The lake itself appears to be a remnant of the last ice age, an indentation left by retreating glaciers. Coltrain and Wood make specific notes about its geography:

> *Haunted Lake has been described as "circular in form," but recent surveys have made its map outline look more like a parallelogram. It is nearly a mile in length (east and west), and nearly five-sixths of a mile in width. It is spoken of as "rather shallow." No doubt in distant years the water was much deeper than now, and higher water than for ages may account for certain peculiarities of its banks as they appear now. The high dike-like deposit on the west side has been called "a lateral Moraine of the glacier period." On the north side there is a portion of what appears like the same*

moraine which has been described as a dike or "bar 20 rods long, six feet high, and three or four feet thick," and also parts of the same appear on the east bank. To many of us this "moraine" explanation is open to doubt, as is any other yet advanced. This is not the place to discuss the matter; but the student of nature may find many things remarkable and suggestive in the environments of Haunted Lake.

Two early legends associated with the lake illustrate the fear that it held for local residents. In 1741, two young men arrived at Francestown from Hillsborough, intending to buy land around the lake. Although they had left separately, they met with each other in the forest and decided to travel together, having the same destination.

Somewhere along the way, however, the relationship between the men seemed to have soured, and an altercation erupted. One of the men ended up killing the other and deposited him in a shallow grave, covered with tree branches. The story is that the man's spirit never rested and can be heard crying and moaning as he desperately tries to make his way out of the forest.

Another tale of violence concerns two hunters from Dunstable, Massachusetts, who determined to try their luck around the lake. Setting up camp west of the Great Meadows in New Boston, they settled into a routine of setting their traps each morning, which they located around the bank of the lake, and then heading up to the south branch of the Piscataquog River. They would take the rounds in turn, meeting up at camp about noon. Coltrain and Wood take up the story:

One day one of them did not return, and after waiting till satisfied there was trouble, the other started on his companion's route, and near this water was startled by the growl of a wild beast, and saw only a few feet ahead a huge catamount standing over the dead and torn body of his comrade. He loaded his gun and shot the savage beast, and then buried his friend as well as he could, and returned to camp. Knowing these savage animals roamed the forest in pairs, and as they were dreaded by all hunters, he returned the next day to Dunstable.

In 1753, the Honorable Matthew Patten, of Bedford, proceeded to make a complete survey of the pond. This project would take several days, and his group was obliged to camp on the shore of the lake. They got more than they bargained for, as the supernatural manifestations for which the area is known began to assert themselves. Coltrain and Wood write:

> *At the time of this incident, whether in 1753 or a little earlier, Patten and his two chainmen, with their assistants, encamped for the night near the outlet of the Pond. Soon after darkness set in, there commenced groanings and shrieks as of a human being in distress, and these continued, most plaintive and affecting, till nearly morning. These chairmen were hardy fellows not accustomed to fear the face of man, but they had some superstition, and some alarm at "signs" and "bad omens," and they could not be persuaded to continue their work, even for an hour. They started at once, in the morning, for their home in Bedford. This event, of course, confirmed previous rumors that the place was "haunted." and established the name, "Haunted Pond." For more than a generation it was known by no other name.*

The lake's reputation didn't deter David Scoby, an immigrant from Belfast, Ireland, from setting up a sawmill on the banks of the river in 1780. While digging the foundation of the mill, the workmen were horrified to discover the skeleton of a young man buried in a shallow grave. This event cemented the lake's legend in the minds of the local population, but Scoby went ahead and built the mill anyway. He operated the business on the site until his death in 1834, upon which it fell to Daniel Fuller, who ran the business until 1860, whereupon the site was abandoned.

As I have previously mentioned, Francestown is a quiet place, and the young people of the community were understandably desperate for diversion. Accordingly, in the early nineteenth century, Scoby's sons took note of the reputation of Haunted Lake and decided to use it for their own amusements. As any haunted area is likely to have its share of amateur ghost hunters, the Scoby boys were determined that they would not go away disappointed. Again, Coltrain and Wood take up the tale:

> *Another tradition is that the "Scoby Boys" were given to frightening certain "liquor-laden loafers," who, having imbibed enough to put the mind into a very meditative and susceptible state, were accustomed to pass by the "dark shades and weird waste of bog-land and water" adjacent, in the "wee sma' hours," and were "helped" to see various "ghosts" and "visions" that were both real and "unco wild." And no doubt this also had a basis of fact, the state of mind of these belated travelers, and the cunning of the "Boys," combining to set afloat various "dreadful representations of dreadful things," so that timid people became half-afraid to pass that way even in clear sunlight. Many people fully believed the whole vicinity to be*

The remains of David Scoby's sawmill, as they look today. *Photograph by the author.*

> *"haunted." But this tradition, after all, does not account for the name, since this was known as "Haunted Pond" long before there were any "Scoby Boys" in this vicinity. They only took advantage of the well-known name to help them carry out their "dreadful" jokes!*

A recent expedition to Haunted Lake revealed that the ruins of the Scoby Mill still stand on the lake's shore. The channel leading upstream from the mill is almost dry, a huge beaver dam having cut off the outflow stream. Consequently, the water level is very high, breaching the banks in several places.

You can still see the old stones and dam that once marked the site of the mill, rising up from the side of the brook. It's an ominous place, abandoned for over a century, with odd indentations in the earth and rocks crumbling into the stream.

Haunted Lake certainly lives up to its name; desolate, dark and foreboding, one can almost hear the cries and moans of its many victims

The site of one of the outlying buildings adjoining David Scoby's sawmill. *Photograph by the author.*

as they beg for release from their earthly bonds. As far as ghosts go, however, it's certainly not the only game in town.

A quick shot down Route 47 brings you into the Crotched Mountain Ski Resort, a favorite spot for those who hanker for a slide down the slopes. Even here, though, the bonhomie of well-to-do recreation is tempered by the spirits of those long dead.

Situated on this property is the Toll Booth Tavern, named after the old toll booth that once stood on the Second New Hampshire Turnpike, which ran straight through this neighborhood.

The place was built in 1800 by John Gibson, a second-generation New Englander, whose family hailed from Ulster, Ireland, and had the distinction of being remote cousins to Queen Victoria. John was born in Merrimack on January 17, 1767. On August 12, 1790, he married Hannah (Brown) Quigley, widow of William Quigley of Francestown, and settled into the community shortly thereafter. He built a small house on a hill east of the location of the present tavern and settled down to domestic life. When the

The Toll Booth Tavern, as it looks today. *Photograph by the author.*

turnpike was constructed, however, he saw a distinct business opportunity and moved the entire house down to its vicinity, whereupon he converted it into a tollhouse.

Two years after opening his tavern, John's wife died, and he remarried the following year to one Mary Gale. This woman changed his fortunes considerably; it was said that she had a remarkable ability in uniting the businesses of a merchant with that of a tavern keeper, and it was through her efforts that John became the wealthiest man ever to reside in Hillsborough County. Naturally, it was understood that an individual of his standing would loom large in politics and commerce, and John Gibson stepped right up to the challenge. During the years from 1814 through 1816, he represented Francestown in the state legislature; additionally, he was one of the directors of the Hillsborough Bank and was heavily involved in various businesses throughout the town. Upon his death on April 26, 1821, it was discovered that his estate was in the enviable position of having a total indebtedness of less than ten dollars.

Gibson's tavern was in a remarkably good location. Situated as it was on the only route between Boston and the cities of Vermont, it became a favored spot among numerous travelers. Coltrain and Wood paint a vivid picture of the establishment during its glory days:

> *The "Gibson Tavern" had quite a reputation in its day, as a place of specially good entertainment of table and pillow, and of "jolly times" and even almost boisterous "good cheer." This large hotel was built on the turnpike in the northwest part of the town, by John Gibson in 1800 and was occupied by him till his death* [1821], *and some years afterward by his widow. In the days before the railroads, when so many heavy teams and crowded stages from Boston passed through this place for Vermont and the towns above, this tavern was a favorite among them all in this vicinity. They would put up a little early, or press on a little late, "to turn in at Gibson's." Much of the time the house was full. Here was also a "large tannery" as it was then called; and with the "toll-gate" and bar and store, and large farm operations employing many hands, there was quite a stir of business here. Oft the "hall was cleared," and there were stirring notes and tripping feet!*

After John Gibson's death, Mary continued to run the tavern for many years. She finally gave it up in 1837, whereupon the building was converted to a private residence, a status it maintained for many years thereafter.

Over time, the tavern began to develop a reputation as a haunted house, with various specters making their presence known to subsequent tenants. On a recent visit to the tavern, I decided to make a tour of the various rooms in the house—and, in the process, managed to scare some of the help.

"I never go into the cellar," a young waitress assured me. "It's just too weird down there."

In 1973, longtime Francestown resident B.J. Carbee lived in the tavern and encountered some extremely weird phenomena while there.

"The house was owned by Jeanne and Donough Prince when I lived there," she said.

> *I lived in a brick addition that had been the servants' quarters. It was attached to the main house, where the bar is now.*
>
> *I never had any encounters with the ghosts in the cellar. If anything, my experience was a little more bizarre.*
>
> *There used to be this wonderful screened-in porch in the back of the house. On one of the sides, there was this large door that led out into the yard. Well, it was a warm summer night, and I was keeping the windows open, enjoying the beautiful setting. All of a sudden, my dog started freaking out, barking and yelling. I had no idea what was going on. Right afterward, I could hear hoof beats coming up the road from the town side, heading*

> *toward Deering. At the same time, I could discern the high-pitched scream of a woman echoing through the night. I grabbed my flashlight and went outside, but there wasn't anything there. By this point, the sound had disappeared, and the dog calmed down. I later told one of my friends about this, but he just said that I was delusional.*

This skeptical friend was about to have one of his own supernatural encounters, however, that would alter his perception of these events.

"When he came over to the house about a month or so later, we were seated in the same place on the porch," Carbee recounted. "Again, the hoof beats were coming down the road. This time, however, we could both hear them. The dog started barking and freaking out again, and we both ran out into the yard but could see nothing."

A little investigation spread some light on the weird events in the house and led to a pretty chilling story:

> *When I asked a few people about what we had experienced, they said that there was an old legend stating that a woman had taken a coach to the tavern to meet her fiancé and arrived only to discover that he was dead. It appears the sounds that we heard were an echo of her coach approaching the tavern and then her screams as she received the horrible news.*

Later that year, one of Carbee's friends was taking pictures of her in an upstairs room in the tavern—only to discover some uninvited voyeurs.

"When we developed the photos, images of people appeared in the background," Carbee said. "They weren't there when we were taking the pictures—they only showed up afterward."

In October 2012, the Conscious Spirit Paranormal Group conducted its own investigation of the building and encountered some interesting entities.

"We detected a couple of entities on the property while we were working there," said Theresa Harlow-Sillanpaa, historian, researcher and founder of the group.

> *All of the female mediums on our team confirmed these presences. First off, the spirit of Hannah, John Gibson's first wife, is felt in the front part of the house, sometimes upstairs but mainly on the first floor. There's a tremendous sense of sadness about this spirit, as she died after living in the house for only two years. It's so unfortunate because she could have had a long and happy life. It's obvious that she was very much in love with her husband.*

The front room in the Toll Booth Tavern, said to be haunted by John Gibson's first wife, Hannah. *Photograph by the author.*

That wasn't the only entity detected by the group, however.

"The other presence we discovered in the house was a black servant, who seems to occupy the landing at the top of the stairs," Harlow-Sillanpaa said. "We got the impression that there is something wrong with his feet. We could only surmise that he had ill-fitting shoes or something to that effect. Of course, it could be related to some kind of injury, but we all felt it was his shoes that were presenting the problem."

Harlow-Sillanpaa also confirmed that the employees of the tavern were somewhat reticent about venturing into the cellar. "They all feel really uncomfortable about going down there," she said.

So, in conclusion, it's not strictly true that nothing ever happens in Francestown. While the town itself seems the epitome of quiet placidity, there is definitely a darker side to this hamlet. The spirits are certainly extremely active, for one thing, and aren't even slightly shy about making their presence known.

6

The Ghosts of Amherst

Walking through the center of Amherst is like traveling back in time a couple of centuries. Huge, ancient houses dot the perimeter of the town common, presided over by the stately old courthouse. But beneath its serene beauty lies a history of brutality and murder, the echoes of which can be felt to this day.

Even the name of the town itself speaks of a legacy of genocide. The town was first chartered in 1728 as Narraganset Number 3. It later became known as Souhegan Number 3. In January 1760, the town was finally chartered as Amherst, named for General Jeffrey Amherst, who was, at that time, commander in chief of the British forces occupying the country. In retrospect, the advisability of according this fellow the honor of naming a town after him is somewhat dubious in light of the fact that his most notable accomplishment was handing out smallpox-infected blankets to local tribes, predicating a massive outbreak of disease and wiping out most of the Native Americans in the vicinity. It would be hard to imagine that their restless spirits wouldn't be occupying the area to this day.

In the eighteenth century, the town was considerably larger than it is today. By 1803, portions of Amherst had been peeled off, becoming the neighboring communities of Milford, Merrimack and Mont Vernon. Amherst became the first seat of Hillsborough County upon its formation in 1769. The central village was the home of the courthouse, replete with a jail, pillory and whipping post. By 1869, however, all county government had been removed to either Manchester or Nashua. The courthouse became simply the town hall, and the jail was demolished.

One of the early notable residents of this town was Horace Greeley (February 3, 1911–November 29, 1872). As a newspaper editor and founder of the Liberal Republican Party, he was an outspoken opponent of slavery. Noted as the originator of the famous phrase "Go west, young man," he founded the *New York Tribune* and, later, the *New Yorker*. He also ran for president in the year of his death. His house still stands in the town on Horace Greeley Road.

THE GREAT JAILBREAK OF 1776

One singular incident stands out in the early history of this town: the great jailbreak of 1776. On the night of November 22, fourteen men, imprisoned in the Hillsborough County jailhouse, were intent on making their escape. They had just been transported there earlier in the day and weren't going to waste any time getting out.

Their crime? Being loyal to the British Crown.

Being a Loyalist during those heady days of the Revolutionary War was a considerable offense, punishable by confiscation of property and imprisonment. The problem was, there just weren't a lot of Loyalists in Massachusetts or New Hampshire. New York, on the other hand, was overloaded and was seeking someplace to put them all.

But first, a little back story. When Amherst became the Hillsborough County seat in 1771, this honor also carried with it the obligation to build a courthouse and a jail. Old Jailhouse Road—the site is still there, but the jail long gone—was chosen for the new facility. Well, perhaps "facility" is too fancy a word for this place, which was basically a windowless log house. Back then, prisoners were responsible for their own keep, including food, clothing and lodging. Obviously, those bereft of friends and family would frequently perish while in custody.

A local man who fell prey to this fate was lawyer Joshua Atherton, a popular and outspoken member of the community. Actually, it was this outspokenness that landed him in hot water. Atherton was a Loyalist, fully convinced that the Continental army was doomed in its struggles against the king.

Admired as he was in Amherst, Atherton was nonetheless the target of animosity from surrounding towns. On September 30, 1774, an armed

Old Jailhouse Road, Amherst, photographed in 1851. The old jailhouse can be seen at left. *Amherst Historical Society.*

mob led by one Matthew Patten of Bedford descended on the Atherton home and thence to Jones Tavern, where interrogations took place. These proceedings ended with cheers from the juries and the witnesses, primarily because Atherton was picking up the bar tab.

But as the clouds of war gathered, things grew more intense. The New Hampshire Committee of Safety and the Continental Congress stepped in. Atherton's barn was burned to the ground. His house was searched for a supposed British spy. In 1776, Atherton was incarcerated at the Amherst jail and then moved, in 1777, to a larger facility in Exeter.

The next year, he was returned to Amherst, in response to local petitions, and was eventually released on a bond of £1,000. The year 1779 saw him taking an oath of allegiance to the new country and released.

Atherton was subsequently sent to Exeter as a delegate to ratify the Constitution. However, he voted against it, as there were no stipulations contained in it opposing slavery, an institution he abhorred.

As popular as Atherton was in Amherst, the men who were imprisoned there in 1776 had no such support systems. They had to make a break for it on their own. Freeing themselves and making their way back to New York, they took the time to compose a little poem in order to humiliate their less-than-successful jailers:

Come all ye people and hear the rout,
The jail is broke and the prisoners are out
Resolving to be free;
So mount your horses, load your guns,
And see you catch them every one,
And bring them back to me.

I heard a man from Wilton say,
That just about the break of day,
As to market he came,
To sell his butter and cheese,
He spied some Tories he believed,
Straight-away marching home.

Pull off for blood and raise the town,
Be careful to waylay the ground
Before they pass by,
Watch every hollow, plain and ridge
And set a guard at every bridge.

For all the people know it round,
That I'm COMMITTEE for our town,
And if these men be lost,
I'll venture fifty pounds to one,
That I shall lose my post.

One would suppose that such an embarrassing incident might have prompted the immediate construction of a new facility, but that didn't occur until 1811, when a two-story granite facility was built on the site. It is thought that the first floor was to house men, the second to lodge women and the attic to store gallows. Prisoners were still expected to provide for themselves, until this practice was abolished in 1818 by one Sheriff Pierce. Additionally, the convicts were allowed a certain amount of liberty during daylight hours, although they were shackled to the prison walls by iron rings at night.

Joshua Atherton's problems didn't end when he pledged allegiance to the nascent nation. The February 24, 1790 edition of the *Concord Herald* recounts a particularly nasty piece of vandalism visited upon him in that year:

The second Amherst jailhouse, photographed in the late nineteenth century. *From* New Hampshire Historical Moments, *2004.*

> *On the night of the 7th ult., some evil-minded person set fire to two barns belonging to an attorney in that town, in which was his hay, grain, &c., which were all consumed by the flames. Four cows perished in the fire. Amongst the ruins were found small earthen pans, containing coals, by which it is supposed the fire was communicated.*
>
> *Another attorney (in the same town) found the next morning the follow laconic advice: "Be ye also ready." A* nota bene *directed him to "Look down." Upon casting his eyes upon the ground he beheld a fagot of pine splinters pitched at the ends. We leave it to the world to guess their meaning.*

In a town the size of Amherst, it didn't take the authorities very long to track down and prosecute the perpetrator. Accordingly, we find the following notice in the May 25, 1790 edition of the same paper:

> *On the 13th inst., at Amherst, Michael Keef was convicted before the Supreme Court on two indictments, one for writing and publishing traitorous and seditious letters; the other for burning a barn, the property of Joshua Atherton, Esq., of said Amherst.*
>
> *For the first offence, he was sentenced to be whipped 15 stripes, and sit on the gallows one hour with a rope around his neck, pay costs of prosecution and stand committed until sentence should be performed. For burning the barn he was sentenced to be whipped 30 stripes, be imprisoned six months from next June, pay costs of prosecution, and stand committed until sentence be performed.*

Keef had no intention of serving out his sentence, however, and was determined to cheat the hand of justice. A graphic description of the desperate measures he took was published in the June 4, 1790 edition of the *Pennsylvania Packet*:

> *PORTSMOUTH (N.H.) May 22. We hear from Amherst, that one Keef, the person who was convicted of setting fire to the barn of Joshua Atherton, Esq.; (by which it was entirely consumed with its contents) and for which he was sentenced by the court to stand in the pillory one hour, and receive 20 stripes—let on the gallows, and receive 30 stripes, on Friday last took an effectual and sure method to evade that punishment which a crime so heinous justly merited. After sentence was passed upon him, he was remanded back to prison, when the gaoler brought him a in a plate of victuals, with a knife and fork, and withdrew. After some time the gaoler returned to see his prisoner, when, shocking to relate, he beheld Keef stretched out on the floor a corpse, with his throat cut from ear to ear! The knife which was brought him to eat his dinner with, he made use of to effect so dreadful a purpose.*

This jail was closed in 1867 and demolished. There are some souvenirs left over from those days, however. The original lock and door of the old jailhouse is on display at the Amherst Historical Society's Wigwam Museum. And you'll still see some of the stones if you stroll down to the intersection of Mack Hill and Manchester Road. There, you'll see the Beaver Brook Bridge, built of those same blocks with the shackling rings still attached. If there are any ghosts extant in the old Amherst jailhouse, they surely haunt this bridge.

"AN AUTHENTICATED GHOST STORY"

Since the dawn of the nineteenth century, the paper of note in this area has been the *Farmer's Cabinet*, located originally in Amherst and later moved to an old schoolhouse in Milford. From 1802 until 2005, this newspaper was owned by the Rotch family, who passed it down through the generations until it was sold to out-of-state concerns.

I actually worked as a writer and editor for this newspaper for a good five years and became intimately acquainted with the area. As mentioned in the introduction to this volume, it was here where Dr. Blood met his ghastly end, courtesy of the spirit of Judith Thompson. It is also here where the Country Tavern is located, hard on Route 101, haunted by the ghost of Elizabeth Ford. But more about that later.

Looking through the archives of this venerable journal, I found the following odd little piece concerning a supposed haunting, dated May 12, 1875. The particulars of the situation seem to be kept deliberately vague, as was the fashion in those days:

> *AN AUTHENTICATED GHOST STORY.*
> *A gentleman had occasion to visit a certain city in New England. He arrived at night, went directly to his bed, slept soundly through the night, and in the morning discovered that his watch had stopped during the night. When he opened the door of his room, another gentleman was taking in his boots on the opposite side of the corridor; and of him our friend asked if he could tell him what time it was. To his surprise the gentleman took no notice whatever of the question. He asked again: "Sir, will you be good enough to tell me what time it is? My watch has stopped." No answer. The gentleman without looking up, shut his door and disappeared. At that moment two other gentlemen came walking together down the corridor; and Mr. X asked the same question. The two gentlemen, without looking right or left, continued their walk without answer or sign. "Well," thought Mr. X, "this is very curious." However, he went back into his room. Presently the bell rang for breakfast; and immediately a waiter entered the room, seized him by the arm, and began a series of gesticulations. Mr. X lost his temper, and burst forth with, "What is the matter?" When the waiter replied "Oh!" and vanished, laughing. Mr. X began to think something was very wrong, but went to breakfast. When he entered the* salle a manger, *which commonly had a dozen or twenty people at the tables, he found the hall filled with gentlemen in black coats, all feeding gravely, and in perfect silence. A waiter silently beckoned him to*

a place, and when he was seated, he said to his neighbor, "Sir, will you be kind enough to tell me what this is all about?" No answer. The person, like Charlotte "Werter," went on eating bread and butter. Our friend, too, began to feel decidedly what the English call queer, and getting out of his seat, went to the nearest waiter, and piteously besought him for Heaven's sake to tell him what was the matter with this house. "Oh!" said the waiter, "don't you know? Why, this is the Deaf and Dumb Convention that meets to-day in Hartford."—Old and New.

THE GHOST OF ELIZABETH FORD

Whimsical as the "Authenticated Ghost Story" piece is, there are spirits aplenty in this old town. The most famous haunted house is the Country Tavern, formerly a private home, where a spirit walks to this day.

Driving down Route 101A, as it winds through Milford and Amherst on its way to Nashua, one is assailed by a constant succession of strip malls, big-box stores and chain restaurants. The traffic is crazy here—people constantly switch lanes without turning on their signals, overtake one another seemingly at random and utilize their car horns liberally.

Go back a couple hundred years, however, and you would have found a completely different picture. Farms and forests would have stretched as far as the eye could see, and the only sounds would have been the chirping of birds and the rustling of leaves.

There is one remnant of that time: the Country Tavern, a homey restaurant set back from the road, beckoning potential diners with the promise of colonial charm.

This is no piece of New England artifice, luring in hapless tourists with fake pretensions of Old World glamour. No, it's the real thing—a genuine old house dating back to 1741, with a grisly history.

Naturally, it's also haunted.

The ghost is that of Elizabeth Ford, a spirit that playfully has made itself at home in the eating establishment. For many years now, she has been moving cutlery around, misplacing various items and generally making herself known. For all that, she's pretty benign; on only one occasion did she aim a plate at the head of a particularly obnoxious customer.

The ghost is said to be about five and a half feet tall, with long white hair and a flowing white gown.

Above: The Country Tavern in Amherst as it looks today. *Photograph by the author.*

Below: The main dining room of the Country Tavern, where the ghost of Elizabeth Ford is said to be the most active. *Photograph by the author.*

The details of Elizabeth's life are a little fuzzy. After all, Nashua didn't really keep records of the lives of its residents until the nineteenth century. What we can glean from the legend, however, bespeaks a brief life tinged with tragedy and murder.

In order to understand the history of her life, we have to travel back to 1741, when one Captain Ford, a seaman of English extraction, decided to settle in the area and build a home for himself and his vivacious twenty-two-year-old wife.

Apparently, there were problems right from the start. For one thing, Elizabeth's husband was many years her senior; secondly, his voyages could take him away from home for many years at a time. This left the girl alone in the huge house, bored and in desperate need of company.

The trouble really started when Captain Ford undertook a long sea voyage, which took him away from the house for a good ten months. Upon his return, he discovered that his bride had given birth to a child—one that he could not have possibly fathered. Enraged, he locked Elizabeth in the cellar for a good two days as she cried and pleaded for the life of her progeny.

Eventually, the captain returned to the cellar. He informed his wife that he had killed the baby and disposed of the body on the grounds.

Elizabeth immediately flew into a violent rage and attacked her husband. As they struggled, he stabbed her to death.

Captain Ford now had another body to deal with. In desperation, he decided to dump it down the well in the back of the house.

The bulkhead leading to the cellar of the Country Tavern, where Elizabeth Ford was allegedly murdered by her husband. *Photograph by the author.*

What became of the captain isn't really recorded, but the legend of Elizabeth, wandering around the house in search of her lost child, lives on. The residence was converted into a restaurant back in the 1980s, a function it retains to this day. The change in venue hasn't slowed Elizabeth down one bit, however, and she is still a prominent fixture in the house as ever.

"I'm actually a bit of a skeptic," said John Randall, manager of restaurant. "So I've never seen anything here that would lead me to believe in ghosts. On the other hand, there have been so many other people who have experienced things that I just can't really throw it out."

Randall says that the ghost of Elizabeth Ford has excited a great deal of attention from the local media and paranormal investigation societies. "We've been here for fifteen years, and the stories go back many years before us," he said. "We had one of these investigation groups come in here at night with their recording equipment and infrared cameras, and they said they found a lot of things."

An old *Nashua Telegraph* story from several years ago by Judith M. Bennett recounted an experience by former restaurant manager Bonnie Gamache, who was also initially a skeptic. "I make no bones about it that I thought this ghost business was a bit of bunk at the beginning," she said at the time. "But one day, a family from Virginia, who used to live in this house, came in to eat and spoke fondly of Elizabeth playing with their young son. The son, now a thirty-five-year-old attorney, was with them and corroborated all this. I began to believe it all then."

Randall says the "hot spot" of the haunting is located in the bathrooms and dining room of the upstairs section of what used to be the barn. "Some of the staff will see a shadow up there or something brushing by them," he said. "One customer was seated for dinner and actually saw the salt and pepper shakers moving across the table."

Although deteriorated by the centuries, the sites of the crimes are still clearly visible. The apple tree under which Captain Ford allegedly buried the baby was extant until relatively recently. "That apple tree was as old as the house," said Randall. "It was such a centerpiece of the property that the previous owners did all they could to preserve it. They put cement in the base of the tree where it was rotting out and tied it down with cables. Then, about ten or eleven years ago, a storm came through and blew the whole thing down. You can still see the stump and the cement base, though."

And what of the old well, where Elizabeth was said to have been dumped after her murder? "It's still out there," said Randall, "next to the road that

The old well on the property of the Country Tavern, where Captain Ford was said to have deposited the body of his wife after the murder. *Photograph by the author.*

leads out to the airport. It's covered by a plank and pretty much filled in. But you can still see it."

Occasionally, the ghost has been observed gazing wistfully out of the barn windows into the yard, where her baby was buried.

Randall took me on a tour of the grounds, where I shot some photos of the remnants of the apple tree marking the grave of the child and the site of the well where Elizabeth's remnants are said to lie. Then we went into the upstairs dining room, the area where the haunting was said to be at its most intense. There, I shot four photographs of the room. The first three were completely clear, but the fourth showed evidence of "orbs"; that is, spherical blobs of light generally associated with psychic phenomena.

Over the years, various groups of psychic investigators have conducted examinations of the house and confirm that there are entities walking here. One of these is a medium by the name of April Sheerin, who has operated the New Millennium Psychic Center in Derry since 1998.

Among the entities observed by Sheerin is a man in dark clothing who apparently hanged himself in the main dining room. This leads one to wonder: could this be the specter of Captain Ford, whose fate remains unknown? It is after all possible that, struck by remorse over the murder of his wife, he took his own life in the house.

Another more identifiable spirit is that of Elizabeth herself, which sometimes resides in the cellar where she was murdered, crying out for her lost child. Sheerin has said that she senses an intense feeling of melancholy in this area.

The owners of the tavern aren't shy about talking about Elizabeth; she is, after all, a major source of publicity for the restaurant itself, and her spectral shenanigans are not in the least threatening. One hopes, however, that someday she will be reunited with her child and find some kind of rest.

THE CAPTAIN AND THE MONKEY

The last entry in this chapter is a piece of whimsicality, a breath of fresh air in the midst of all of this horror and murder. It comes to us, once again, courtesy of the *Farmer's Cabinet*, published in its October 8, 1811 edition:

> *A Captain…went into company with several other gentlemen to lodge in an inn, the keeper of which had lost his mother, and she had just been buried. There was in the house a monkey, which used often to divert the deceased. In the evening, the master of house having sent one of the servants up into the chamber where his mother died, in order to fetch some linen; the servant came running down, out of breath, crying out that he had seen his mistress, that she was come again, and was now lying on the bed. Another of the servants, who fancied he had more courage, went up and returned in the same manner, asserting positively that she was in the bed. The master of the house resolved to take with him one of the maids with a light. Immediately, he came down in a violent hurry, and cried out to the gentlemen, who were at supper, "Yes, gentlemen, it is too true, my poor mother, there she is; I saw her myself, but had not sufficient courage to speak to her; for God's sake, go up and be witnesses to the truth of what I say." The captain observed no one offered to stir, took a candle, and addressed himself to a Dominican friar, who was one of the company, "Come, father," says he, "let you and I go together." "With all my heart," replied the friar, "provided you go foremost"; and accordingly they went up with each a candle in his hand; and now the rest of the company and even the master of the house and the servants would*

> *go up with them. When they had got to the room; and had drawn away the curtains, the officer discovered the figure of an elderly black woman, much wrinkled, looking boldly at them, and making ridiculous grimaces, as if she meant to laugh at them. Upon this they bade the innkeeper to come forward, and see whether it was his mother. "Ah!" answered he, "it is she, it is my poor dead mother!" The servants too all asserted that it was their mistress. The officer then desired the Dominican, as he was a priest, to speak to her, and ask her business. The friar began with "Who are you? What would you have?" and at the same time besprinkled the spectre with holy water; but his hand trembling for fear, he was uncommonly liberal in the quantity. The monkey, at this, quitted the bed, and leapt upon the friar's head, who began to make off, crying out with all his might; the animal in the mean time biting and scratching his pate. The friar took to the door, and the rest of the company followed his example; but the officer, who was last, saw plainly that it was nothing but a monkey in a woman's headdress. The friar bestirred himself so effectually, that at last he shook off the monkey, and the animal in falling, dropped its headdress, and was immediately known by the family. Thus the whole scene terminated in a laugh, and it was found that the monkey, having often seen his mistress dress her head, had taken a fancy to imitate her, and then had laid down in the bed where she died.*

The quiet demeanor of the town of Amherst belies its bloody history. One can almost hear the cries of the natives who were decimated by disease, the victorious whoops of newly liberated Tories and their frustrated jailers and the ghost of poor Elizabeth, doomed forever to seek her murdered child.

7
MERRIMACK'S RESTLESS SPIRITS

We now turn our attentions to the town of Merrimack, a community sitting hard on the Merrimack River. Europeans first settled here in the late seventeenth century, and for a time, it was incorporated into the largely disputed designation of Old Dunstable, which was a matter of contention between the Province of New Hampshire and the Massachusetts Bay Colony.

The town was incorporated in 1746, named after a kind of sturgeon that once proliferated in the area. The Penacook Indians spelled it *Monnomoke* or *Merramake*. The town took on a different spelling, Merrymac. At that time, only the southern boundaries of the town were included, specifically the area known as Thornton's Ferry. The northern portion of the town, Reed's Ferry, was added into the mix a few years later.

Naturally, a town of this age and pedigree has engendered its own share of spirits. Here, we will turn our attention to a couple particularly notoriously haunted houses.

In the February 24, 1827 edition of the *Merrimack Journal*, there is published a piece entitled "Montville; or the Haunted House, a Legend of the Merrimack," penned by one Francis Le Pedane. It tells of one of the earliest settlers in this area, an immigrant from England, who built a palatial mansion on the side of the river. In time, however, his prosperous lifestyle was brought low by the apparition of a particularly unpleasant specter:

His house was built upon a rising ground, and commanded one of the finest prospects of the Merrimac. It was constructed in a style of splendor far surpassing any which the colonists had then reared, and the combination of the various orders of architecture, a knowledge of which he had brought with him from England, excited the admiration and astonishment of those who had never beheld the gorgeous magnificence displayed upon some of the private as well as public buildings of the more polished nations of the old world. He had brought with him from England all the furniture necessary to furnish his house in a princely manner, and his tables might almost be said to be burdened with the masses of silver of which they were loaded. His household was composed of man-servants and maid-servants, but yet there was one thing wanting to give him dignity and respectability in his retirement, a wife.

Here our history suffers an interruption for the want of well-authenticated facts. But a few years had rolled away when the scene appears to be entirely changed. He whose every step was the movement of hilarity, and whose company was sought for those for whom wealth and its appendages had any attractions, was prostrate upon his couch, in his almost deserted palace, the subject of the most excruciating torments, of bodily pains and mental anguish. To relieve his sufferings was beyond the art of the most skilful physicians. His robust form gave way to the burthens that oppressed it, and his healthful countenance became sallow, sunk and dejected. To rise from his bed and gaze upon his extensive domain from his window afforded him no satisfaction. The ground to him looked parched with drought, the green grass seemed withered, the trees blighted, and the cheerful sun was steeped in blood. Night came but to be a witness to his mental anguish. His dreams were fraught with circumstances too horrid for description, and often he would be aroused by the wailings of distress; sometimes he would see by his bedside a maiden holding over him a large knife reeking with blood, bearing on her bosom an infant black with suffocation; at one moment threatening him with instant destruction and again pouring forth the holy incense of a broken heart in appeals to his better feelings. He would spring from his bed and order his servant to thrust that maniac girl out of doors, and then storm at the supposed insolence of the poor fellow who could discern nothing but his master. At length to relieve himself from the wretchedness of his situation if possible, he determined on quitting his costly habitation, which seemed to him to have become the abode of devils, and accordingly took up his residence in a neighboring cottage.

His house with all its splendors became desolate. The traveler was often frightened by the unearthly sounds that proceeded from it, and the village maiden would cling more closely to her lover as they passed it with a quickened pace in a moonlit evening. At length it went to decay—Montville found no relief by his change of residence. The same awful sounds would break upon his silence, and the same demoniacal specters haunted him. Worn out and exhausted he expired in a fit of phrenzy [sic], *a sad spectacle of the effects produced by the combined power of imagination and a guilty conscience on human nature.*

So passed way the glory of the House of Montville. His estate was long ago subjected to innumerable divisions, which have become the property of the industrious yeomen who inhabit the valley of the Merrimac.

It has been further noted that, for many years after, travelers who passed on the Middlesex Turnpike to Boston have had the haunted house pointed out to them and would recognize the sad history of this ruin.

From this tale, we turn to another haunted house, once a landmark on a lonely country road but now sitting on a busy thoroughfare. A popular restaurant, it holds the unique distinction of having been built by one of the men who actually signed the Declaration of Independence.

The Common Man Restaurant in Merrimack, as it looks today. *Loretta Jackson/the* Cabinet Press.

The beam where James Thornton hanged himself in the living room of the Common Man Restaurant. *Loretta Jackson/the* Cabinet Press.

The restaurant in question is the Common Man Tavern, built originally by founding father Matthew Thornton in 1797 as a wedding gift for his son, James, who had married Mary Parker. For over two decades, it has been considered a place of conviviality and hospitality.

James tried to run the place for a few years, but things seemed to just get ahead of him. In the end, he decided to end it all and hanged himself from a beam in the living room. As a matter of fact, you can still see the spot where he died to this day.

Right from the beginning, this neighborhood had a rocky start, according to Anita Creager, president of the Merrimack Historical Society.

"Matthew Thornton may have lived there for a time, but that's not certain," she said. "He had a home of his own, closer to the river. As it was, Matthew Thornton owned that whole part of town."

What is known is that this portion of town was purchased by one Jonathon Cummings, a farmer in Litchfield. He bought eighty-one-acre Lot Number 12 in the 1656 Massachusetts grant of Brenton Farm from the estate of Sandy Calley. In December 1763, he sold the property to Colonel Edward Goldstone Lutwyche, who established a ferry crossing across the Merrimack in 1767.

When hostilities broke out between the colonists and the Crown in April 1775, Lutwyche unfortunately found himself on the wrong side of the conflict, at least as far as his neighbors were concerned. As the rebels engaged the redcoats at Concord Bridge, he refused to call out his regiment, and on the evening of April 20, he snuck out of the house, leaving his mother, Sarah, behind, and scooted behind British lines in Boston. He never returned.

As far as the colonists were concerned, this was tantamount to treason. Consequently, the committee of safety for the towns of Merrimack and Litchfield seized his mother's property on the grounds that it belonged to her son.

Well, Sarah was having none of this. On October 24, 1775, she appealed to the Provincial Congress, then in session in Exeter, and prevailed; on November 2, it ordered the property, along with all intermediate profits, to be restored to the old lady.

When Sarah died on September 7, 1778, at the age of seventy-seven, the state committee of safety directed a number of local gentlemen—Colonel Nochols, Mr. Underwood and Major Chase—to take a full inventory of the property. In 1780, the whole lot was brought up by Matthew Thornton. Thornton himself had a troubled life. He was born in 1714 in Ireland to James Thornton and Elizabeth Malone. When the boy was but three years old, the family moved to Brunswick, Maine. On July 11, 1722, the community was attacked by Indians, and the family fled the burning home, settling in Worcester, Massachusetts. Years later, Thornton practiced medicine in Londonderry, New Hampshire. In 1745, he was appointed surgeon to the New Hampshire Militia, and in 1760, he married Hannah Jack, with whom he had five children. At the outbreak of war, he was a member of the committee of safety and drafted the first constitution in the United States, effectively dissolving ties to the royal government.

According to Creager, there is a certain amount of evidence that the Thorntons did actually care for Sarah in her declining years.

"If you look in the family plot, you'll see that Sarah's grave is right there next to the Thorntons," she said. "There's no real evidence that she was cared for by them, but the fact that the grave is right there implies so."

So it's relatively obvious that Thornton was a major player in New Hampshire politics at this time. When he built the tavern as a wedding present for his son, James, the family was one of the richest and most influential clans in the area. One can only speculate on what drove the young man to take his own life a few short years later.

Tragedy seemed to follow the Thornton family through the generations. Consider, for instance, this sad little piece reported in the *Salem (MA) Observer* in its August 10, 1850 edition:

> *Melancholy Death: Miss Margaret Ann Thornton, of Thornton's Ferry, N.H., a grand daughter of Old Matthew Thornton, one of the signers of the Declaration of Independence, arrived at Albany on Wednesday on her way home from Jackson, Mississippi, where she had charge of a female academy. On Friday morning she sent for a bottle of chloroform, and retired to her room. Not making an appearance as late as 2 o'clock in the afternoon, the door was forced open, and she was found dead, with every indication of having taken an overdose of chloroform; it was supposed that it was taken to allay pain, either the effect of the disease or of the drugs she had before taken.*

The last of Matthew Thornton's direct descendants, James Shepherd Thornton, died on May 14, 1875, having distinguished himself in the Civil War. The *Portsmouth Journal of Literature and Politics* published the following account on January 8, 1876:

> *CAPT. THORNTON—The widow of the late Capt. James S. Thornton has erected a marble monument over his remains, at Merrimack, in the new cemetery, a few rods from the church, near Souhegan Village. It is of Italian marble, six and one half feet in height, and consists of a cross resting on a granite base. The inscription is as follows:*
>
> *James Shepard Thornton, Capt. U.S. Navy, Born Feb. 25th, 1827, Died May 14th, 1875.*
>
> *Executive officer of the flag ship* Hartford, *in the naval battles at New Orleans; and on the Mississippi river, and also, of the* Kearsage *in the naval action with the* Alabama.
>
> *Capt. Thornton is the last of the descendents bearing the name of Matthew Thornton, one of the signers of the declaration of independence from New Hampshire. His father died at Valparaíso in 1838, in the public service, being Minister to Chili. He was buried in Valparaíso; Capt. Thornton removed his remains to Merrimack two or three years ago. His mother died several years ago. His sister, wife of Judge Wm. S. Gardner, of Newton, Mass., survived him only a few weeks, leaving two children.*

Matthew Thornton himself had a somewhat belated honor bestowed on him by the State of New Hampshire, as a memorial was dedicated to the veteran in 1892. The *Springfield (MA) Republican* reported on the ceremony in its September 30 edition:

> *MONUMENT TO MATTHEW THORNTON.*
> *Dedicated with Interesting Exercises at Merrimack, N.H.*
> *The dedication of the Matthew Thornton monument erected by the State of New Hampshire and the town of Merrimack to the memory of Matthew Thornton, one of the signers of the Declaration of Independence, took place yesterday afternoon at Merrimack, N.H. There was a large crowd of people at the exercises, which were held in a large tent on the property formerly occupied by Thornton in that part of town called Thornton's Ferry. Gov. Tuttle with his staff and council were present and accepted the memorial in behalf of the state. Gen. C.H. Burns of Nashua was the orator, and his address was an eloquent presentation on the value of patriotism.*

As time went on, the house was inherited by future generations—but not all of them Thorntons.

"The house stayed in the family until the 1970s," said Creager. "But the family intermarried with the Greeleys. As it turned out, some of the generations of the Thornton family didn't have any male descendants, so the Greeley family became the primary owners."

In 1977, the house was bought by Charles Mulch, who renovated it and turned it back into a tavern. According to Creager, he restored much of the original décor and renamed the place the Signer's House.

In the early 1980s, the property changed hands yet again and became the Hannah Jack Tavern, named after Matthew Thornton's wife. Then, about a decade ago, it was acquired by the restaurant chain the Common Man, which runs it to this day.

By this point, you're probably wondering about the ghosts. Well, there's a significant amount of testimony that would seem to confirm their existence.

"I've seen various newspaper reports over the years pertaining to the ghosts," Creager said. "But most of them seem to involve a female spirit."

This would seem to be borne out by the testimony of two former managers of the Common Man. Scott McCann recalled a particularly odd event at the house.

"The last time 'Ghost Hunters' was in Merrimack, I got to do the investigation with them," he recounted.

> *They had about thirty video cameras set up throughout the building, as well as audio equipment. We spent most of the time in the basement because that was where they thought most of the activity was happening. I was sitting down in the basement with my dimly lit hard hat, with about five of the ghost hunters. All of a sudden, we heard what sounded like someone running by. The noise went right past us, and I swear I could feel a slight breeze, as if somebody had just actually run past us. I was a little reluctant to think that this was actually real at first, but then it happened again.*
>
> *At this point, I went upstairs and asked the guy with all the audio equipment if he had managed to record the footsteps and if he could play them back for me. He did so, and sure enough, you could hear the sound of someone running past, clear as day.*
>
> *I went back downstairs and asked the other investigators whom they thought this was, and they said it was probably Matthew Thornton's son, James, who actually killed himself in one of the rooms upstairs.*
>
> *This is the only time I had actually heard anything in my seven years at the Merrimack location. I've been told other stories, about an Indian in the building and a woman in a long black dress who walks up the staircase to the upstairs bar. A past employee, a woman named Ginger Monroe, once said that she once encountered a little girl in the kitchen who was complaining that she was lost. The girl was so upset that Ginger called the police. When she got back to the kitchen, the girl was gone. I'm not sure what exactly she said to the police when they arrived, but I can only imagine what was going through their heads.*

Ginger Monroe had another encounter with the spirits on Father's Day 2007. She was waiting on guests in one of the dining rooms. She filled their water glasses and started serving another table while the first couple went downstairs to the buffet.

As she was introducing herself to the other guests, she suddenly heard a loud crash behind her and turned just in time to see the glasses she had just filled tumble to the floor. The guests at the second table said they had seen them jump off the table.

It doesn't stop there. Another former manager, Jaime Saxe, who is now the general manager of the Ashland branch of the Common Man, also recalled his own paranormal experiences in the house.

"When we first opened, I was setting up the liquor storage room by the cage," he recounted.

> *I heard a woman humming from around the corner—this was the area that the Underground Railroad came through. I double checked and found nobody there. I could very distinctly hear a woman humming three notes.*
>
> *Months later, I was telling this story to one of the bartenders and a cook as we were closing up. We all walked downstairs to leave when I went back, as I had to turn off one more light. As I went into the old carriage house, I heard the same humming. I thought the staff were playing a practical joke on me and went into the kitchen to tell them how "funny" they were being. They weren't there—they were waiting for me outside.*
>
> *We locked up the house and were talking in the parking lot about how strange this was and continued recounting the experiences we had heard in the restaurant when we heard a loud crash from inside the house. We had been outside for a good ten minutes, but the pans had started to fall over. Needless to say, I did not go on that side of the basement alone again. There most certainly was some kind of energy on that side of the building.*

According to Saxe, things being moved or falling over was pretty much a common occurrence in the house:

> *I remember bartending downstairs and talking to the guests about some of these experiences. Dishes started falling over, as well as a couple of bottles. At the same time, upstairs, glasses flipped over on that bar as well. Our bartender said he saw a glass flip off the table and land on the floor without anybody being near it.*
>
> *People would sometimes come into the restaurant who claimed to be sensitive to spirits and said the place was haunted, and I agree.*
>
> *We had another bartender, named Mark, who had worked there back when it was the Hannah Jack Tavern. He said he saw a man in nineteenth-century clothing and a long black coat. Mark said he had never been a believer until that time. When we were opening, I was scrubbing the fireplace and thought I saw a man standing by the doorway.*

Saxe believes that the spirits become more active when people are discussing their activities.

"Things seemed to happen more and more when we would talk about the ghosts," he recalled. "I don't think they like being discussed. We once had a call from someone claiming to be from the show *Ghost Hunters*, and the phone would just keep disconnecting halfway through the call."

The old brick fireplace in the dining room of the Common Man Restaurant. *Loretta Jackson/the* Cabinet Press.

Given the long and strange history of this house, it's hardly surprising that restless spirits would still stalk its halls. One thing is for sure: if you have dinner at the Common Man, you might find that your meal comes with a large side dish of the paranormal.

8

The Spirits of Peterborough and Hancock

It would be difficult to imagine a more serene and artistic town than Peterborough. Nestled in the side of Temple Mountain, bisected by the Contoocok River and Nubanusit Brook, the place was first issued a grant in 1737 and was permanently settled in 1749. Although the settlement wasn't directly attacked by the local Indians, that was always a real and frightening possibility. By 1759, there were fifty families in residence at the spot. The town was incorporated in 1760 by Governor Benning Wentworth, being named after Lieutenant Peter Prescott of Concord.

These days, the town is a burgeoning little arts community, something of a throwback to the arts communities that thrived in this state in the 1960s and '70s. There are small boutiques with jewelry, paintings and handmade fabrics. It's like a time-locked hippie enclave, with creativity and innovation at the forefront.

Even here, though, there is a dark underbelly to the community, as weird events are passed down through folklore. Many of these anecdotes were recounted in an address delivered at the centennial celebration of the town on October 24, 1839, by one John Hopkins Morison. For instance, he stated that early in the town's settlement, there was in residence a small, withered woman by the name of Mrs. Stinson, whom the locals believed resolutely to be a witch. One tale recounts how a cat was seen to be acting strangely in the town and was doused with hot water. Almost immediately, Mrs. Stinson was besieged by a particularly bad case of St. Anthony's fire. It was also recorded that a man in the vicinity of the nearby town of Sharon was plagued by a crow, at which he shot, with little effect. The bird merely wheeled above his head, laughing mockingly. Finally, he tore a silver sleeve button from his coat, loaded it into his gun and fired it at his tormentor, breaking a wing. Again, Mrs. Stinson was afflicted with lameness in one of her arms. These events of sympathetic animal magic seemed to occur over and over again throughout Mrs. Stinson's life. When she finally passed away in the late eighteenth century, it was said that she was little more than a skeleton. Nevertheless, the strong pallbearers who conveyed her to her grave stated that they were "almost crushed to the earth by the weight of sin, and their shoulders remained for weeks black and blue."

Another tale of supposed witchcraft in the town involved a girl by the name of Hannah Scott, who felt she had been bewitched by an old woman by the name of Aspy from the neighboring town of Hancock. For more than a month, this child lay in her bed, unable to open her eyes. The physicians were of no help in alleviating her peculiar malady, and the girl insisted over and over that if Aspy came to bless her, she would recover. At length, the woman came to her bedside and laid her hands over her forehead, intoning, "Your God bless you, and my God bless you." Immediately, her eyes sprang open, the curse lifted.

We now turn to the tale of Baker Moore, one of the few slaves in this town, who was noted for his adeptness with the fiddle. This skill, however, he attributed more to the intervention of the devil than to his own talent. From the December 4, 1845 edition of the *Farmer's Cabinet*, we have the following description of the man, taken from a portrait:

> *A short time since passing through Peterborough, we noticed in the stage tavern the portrait of a jolly looking son of Africa. The eyes were well put in, the wool well put on, and the colors, being all of the darkest, were properly mixed and applied with a strong and skilful hand so that the portrait was natural as life and black as the ace of spades the inscription attached to the picture we copied. It read as follows: "The original of the above portrait was Baker Moore, who was born in Boston in 1755, and brought to Peterborough in 1763, as a slave. At the age of 22 he purchased his freedom for $200, which he never felt himself obliged to pay, nor was it ever exacted. He died in January 1839, aged 84."*

More details on Moore's life are found in *The History of the Town of Peterborough, Hillsborough County, New Hampshire* (1876), written by Albert Smith, MD:

> *All this was religiously believed. And we in our day have known one who, to his dying hour, firmly believed that he had twice been honored by a personal interview with the devil. Old Baker—what child in Peterborough within the last sixty years has not danced to his fiddle, with an ecstasy which no other music ever gave? Who does not remember the benevolent, complacent smile with which his honest, black face and white teeth and eyes shone, as raising his instrument to his chin, and producing the first sweet notes, he looked about on the delighted children that were listening or romping round him? But when we knew him, the minstrel was infirm and old, and now he is gone—light may the turf rest upon his bosom. Such men are like fossil remains and petrifactions, which preserve the exact lineaments of plants and animals centuries perhaps after the living species has become extinct. Their minds receive in youth the impressions then current, and there remain fixed through life; so that Baker, in these matters, may be considered a fair sample of the belief which prevailed sixty or seventy years ago. It was seldom that he could be induced to speak upon the subject, and then with symptoms of terror which it would be difficult to describe. I remember, however, to have heard him once, after casting round a fearful look to be sure that the doors were shut, and the evil spirit not actually in the room. As he was driving the cows to pasture, he said, one evening he met a man who very kindly accosted him, and in the course of the conversation told his fortune, mentioning things that no mortal could have known. He gave him a book, with the request that he would read it. Baker took the book; but it hung like lead upon his spirits. He carried it constantly with him, for he was afraid to leave it behind, and at last, having met "the man" again on horseback, in the north-west part of the town, he returned the book; whereupon the man's eyes glistened like fire, his cloven foot appeared, and he was terribly angry. Baker looked up a moment after and he was gone.*

It's but a short drive of a few miles down the road to the small town of Hancock. This town started as an unidentified settlement on the Contoocook River. First settled in 1764, the town was set off from Peterborough and incorporated in 1779, named in honor of John Hancock, who owned 1,875 acres of land in the community. Hancock was the first governor of the state of Massachusetts, president of the Continental Congress and most well known as the prominent signer of the Declaration of Independence.

Hancock is a veritable time capsule of New England history. Almost every building on Main Street is listed on the National Register of Historic Places as part of the Hancock Village Historic District. The meetinghouse is home to Paul Revere's number 236 bell, which chimes on the hour, day and night. The town doesn't have any paved sidewalks, but gravel paths lead from home to home.

As might be expected from an old Yankee settlement, it also has its odd quirks. One of these involves the institution of the town coffin. You see, the people of this town, given their legendary frugality, decided that they would create a coffin that would be used for the interment of the various indigents and transients who would have the misfortune to shuffle off this mortal coil within the limits of the town borders.

The thing of it was, however, that this was an early example of extreme recycling. The poor soul who occupied this box was taken to the potter's field and unceremoniously dumped into a makeshift grave. The coffin was then taken back to the town's tramp house, where it would be used for the burial of the next poor soul to expire in the town.

Incidentally, it was also used for those citizens of the town who had inconveniently perished during the middle of winter, when it was impossible to dig a grave.

The town coffin now occupies a place of honor in the Hancock Historical Society, a venerable old building on the corner of Main Street and Bennington Road, once owned by Christy H. and Helen C. Duncan. There, it entertains the tourists who come to view this odd piece of New England history.

Until recently, there was a house in this town that was said to be host to a number of spirits. This was the David Hubbard House, built in 1782. The house stood at the end of a dirt road, without any electricity, gas or running water. Over the years, it fell into disuse; it began to develop a reputation as a haunted spot and was a prime target for vandals. Sadly, the house itself was demolished sometime after 2005, and a new house was built on the site.

In 1959, historian Robert Harrington Nylander published an account of this property and the restless ghosts that inhabit it.

According to Nylander, Hubbard was born in Concord in 1754, the son of Ebenezer and Hephzibah (Estabrook) Hubbard. He signed up in the Continental army during the Revolution but was discharged in 1776, owing to his ill health. In 1777 or 1778, he married one Mary Bennett and settled in Hancock the next year, occupying land given to him by his brother-in-law, Charles Barrett. There, he built a small house with a central chimney. Over the next three years, his fortunes increased, and in 1782, he built a much larger residence.

Initially, Hubbard did very well in the tiny community; he served as selectman in 1783 and 1784 and became constable in 1786. Unfortunately, the ensuing years saw his wealth diminish drastically, and by 1792, the selectmen were hounding him for back taxes.

In 1796, Hubbard suddenly disappeared, and a search party was sent out to find him. All they discovered, however, was his hat, found on the shore of Greenfield Pond. His friends dragged the waters, but there was no sign of a body.

In the wake of her husband's disappearance, Mrs. Hubbard returned to Concord with her six children. As an interesting side note, one of the couple's sons, Ebenezer Hubbard, was instrumental in the construction of the Minuteman Statue in 1873, having left $1,000 in his will for that effort.

The house then fell to one Lieutenant Ebenezer Knight, who acquired the property in 1797 and remained in residence until his death in 1815.

In 1816, the house became a den of counterfeiters, who plied their illicit trade from the building. This is where the tales of haunting begin. As Nylander recounts it:

> *It is in connection with this group that the "haunted house" legend arises. In the early days it was usual for travelers to stop at the house for a night's lodging. The travelers were made comfortable, but about midnight they heard dreadful sounds like rattling chains, shrieks, or groans. Upon inquiry, they learned that the occupants had heard nothing unusual. Doubtless any visitor called but once!*
>
> *The next nameless occupants were a family consisting of a father, his daughter, and stepmother. The father, apparently a trader, was frequently away for long periods of time. It was during these times that the mother shut the girl in the dark, damp cellar. Upon one such occasion the child did not cry as usual. The woman ordered her up, but the child replied, "I do not wish to. It is all light down here; Mama is with me." This frightened the woman so that she thought the house was haunted and insisted on moving away.*

It's really rather sad that the David Hubbard House is no longer standing. When it was built, it was thought that this would be the center of town. As the years went on, however, the main street was settled in another area, and the old house was forgotten.

As there were no electric or municipal services supplied to the old mansion, it disappeared into memory and rotted away in the woods. In 1959, historian Robert Harrington Nylander took up residence in the building, performed some renovations and wrote about it in the journal *Old Time New England.*

Upon Nylander's death in 1987, the house once again fell into disuse and was gradually reclaimed by the forest until its eventual demolition nearly twenty years later.

Nobody really likes to talk about the David Hubbard House these days; few people know it even existed.

Like many of these New England towns, Hancock likes to keep its secrets largely to itself. There's a grain of truth in the supposition that the people of this region are pretty much closed mouthed about their history. When the subject of ghosts comes up, they're even more reticent to discuss the topic. Whatever secrets Hancock has, one is unlikely to discern them from the locals. In short, it's a bit like that old Bob and Ray radio skit; as far as many are concerned, "you can't get there from here."

9

Bits and Bobs

Throughout the writing of this book, I have attempted to restrict each chapter to a particular region in Hillsborough County and focus on the paranormal phenomena to be found in those areas. This approach, while enabling the reader to understand how the places in question have become haunted, does leave some loose ends. There are some places that, while haunted, simply do not have the "legs" to enable the construction of a complete chapter. Therefore, I will endeavor to tie up some of these loose ends and focus on some obscure but nonetheless haunted spots that have fallen through the cracks.

The Spirits of Blood Cemetery

One the first sites I would like to address is Pine Hill Cemetery, located on a quiet country road in the small town of Hollis, which sits hard on the Massachusetts border. Locally, this burying place is rather ominously known as "Blood Cemetery," so named after the Blood family, who were among the earliest settlers in this town.

The actual hauntings seem to focus around one grave—that of Abel Blood, who was interred here in 1867. The stone shows a finger, pointing up to the heavens, with Blood's name inscribed beneath. Legend has it that at sundown, the finger will suddenly turn and instead aim straight at the depths of hell. Rumors have grown that Abel was an occultist and worshipped

Satan. Actually, it turns out, he was a devout Christian, and the stories are unfounded. That hasn't stopped vandals from attacking his grave, however, and it has been severely damaged. According to Eric Perry of the Central New Hampshire Paranormal Society, the stone was actually removed to an undisclosed location in order to prevent further desecration.

The cemetery has a long and strange history. It stands on land that one Benjamin Parker Jr. donated back in 1769. He had to sell his farm, and the area became one of the first burial grounds in the new town. Nearly three hundred people have been buried there in the centuries since, and a lot of the graves are now unmarked, their occupants lost to history.

The original Blood family member to settle in the area was Elefan, who was born in Groton, Massachusetts, in 1717. In 1740, he moved to Hollis, where he took up work as a plumber. He married Elizabeth Boynton in 1741 and enlisted as a soldier in the French and Indian War.

Several generations of the Blood family lived in the area for the next several hundred years, the vast majority of them being buried at Pine Hill. Most of them resided at the Blood Farm, which was situated, appropriately enough, on nearby Blood Road. One of them, Nathan Blood, was killed at the Battle of Bunker Hill.

Abel Blood, who has been mentioned previously, seems to have not taken to the other world that easily. It is said that his ghost still wanders the grounds, searching for his wife, Betsy. Paranormal investigators who have toured the site have reported various orbs being caught in photographs, as well as spectral voices recorded on EVPs.

Another persistent legend of the cemetery involves a tale of a family that was allegedly murdered in the area in the late nineteenth century. As the clan was being slaughtered, the youngest member of the family, a boy, fled the house, only to be shot in the back. To this day, travelers in the area report seeing his spirit running out into the road and frantically flagging down passing cars.

Other phenomena include car engines cutting out right in front of the burial ground and cameras suddenly ceasing to work.

Over the years, the cemetery has attracted more than its share of attention. As a matter of fact, there is even a website dedicated to the area—www.bloodcemetery.com—which sports a number of photographs, as well as personal accounts of phenomena at the site.

It should be noted that, due to this notoriety, the local police are extremely attentive to the cemetery and will prosecute any unwanted visitors they find after sundown, especially around the time of Halloween.

A MESSAGE FROM BEYOND THE GRAVE

Moving over to Nashua, we find an account of an odd case of premonition in the horrific November 12, 1954 train crash that took place in the center of the city, injuring nineteen people and killing one. It seems that the train came in at an excessive speed at 5:50 a.m. and crashed into two parked freight cars, pushing them through the wall of the Johns Manville Co. warehouse opposite the station. According to a report from the Associated Press, Mail Clerk Lester Hyde, of Medford, Massachusetts, noted, "There was an awful lot of noise. Five or six of us in the mail car were tossed around like ten pins. We were in the car for about a half hour before anyone could get to us."

Richard Stinchfield of Hudson, who worked in the warehouse, further testified, "I rushed from the building and saw the cars toppled over on the left side. There were screams from the inside of the cars. With a group of men I boarded the train and carried the victims out."

The sole fatality in this cataclysm was thirty-five-year-old Mrs. Mary Buckley, a mother of five. It was the sad duty of her husband, Walter, to break the news of her mother's death to their daughter Catherine, who was only eleven years old and also a passenger on the train. As it turned out, however, the child mysteriously already knew of her mother's fate. We have the following account from the Sunday, November 14 edition of the *Boston Advertiser*:

> *Girl Sensed Mother's Train Crash Death*
> *MANCHESTER, N.H.—An ailing 11-year-old girl's sad suspicions were confirmed here yesterday when her grief stricken father disclosed to her that her mother had been killed in Friday's derailment of a Boston & Maine express train at Nashua.*
>
> *It was a heartbreaking task for Walter Buckle, of Laurel St., to tell his daughter, Catherine, the tragic news but his sad duty was made somewhat easier by the fact that the child had feared the worst ever since she lost contact with her mother at the time of the wreck.*
>
> *Catherine was being taken to the Children's Medical Center in Boston by her mother, Mrs. Mary Buckley, 35, to treat an undisclosed ailment when the accident occurred.*
>
> *At Memorial Hospital, Nashua, the child cried for her mother, then suddenly stopped. Attaches said she seemed to realize her mother was gone. Her father came to her bedside but was unable to steel himself to tell her the sad news until yesterday.*

He had to bring the same sad tidings to four other children when he returned home from the hospital with Catherine after her release.

Meanwhile, the Boston & Maine, which suspended the fireman and engineer of the Red Wing, the crack Montreal–Boston express as a routine measure after a serious accident, prepared to open a probe of the crash at Concord tomorrow.

Separate probes of the crash are also being conducted by the New Hampshire Public Utilities Commission and the Interstate Commerce Commission.

The suspended men are Engineer Samuel J. Burns, 62, of Oak Point Rd., Saugus, Mass., and Fireman J.P. Llaflamme, 64, of Nashua. At his Saugus home, Burns refused to comment on the matter, saying he had been instructed to make no statements until railroad attorneys had conferred with him.

A Boston & Maine spokesman said such suspensions are routine after a serious accident and added that the Nashua derailment was the road's worst passenger train accident in 36 years.

THE HAUNTED SANDWICH SHOP

Feeling hungry? Well, if victuals are your only intent, then you could frequent most any submarine joint in Nashua. On the other hand, if you have an appetite for the bizarre, then your best destination would have to be the Sausage King, located on Main Street, a stone's throw from Railroad Square. The thing of it is, though, that before the new owners settled in, the property was originally Rice's Pharmacy, the oldest drugstore in the state of New Hampshire, founded back in 1868. The front of the building was where compounds and tinctures were sold. In the back was a spot where the pharmaceuticals were prepared.

Downstairs, however, it was a completely different story. The area is used for storage now, its bare walls exuding an ominous atmosphere. This is where various operations were performed, everything from dental work to lobotomies, often without the benefit of anesthesia. One can only imagine the amount of pain that people had to endure in nineteenth-century medical procedures and the amount of screaming that accompanied it.

According to the present staff, that just didn't stop. In the middle of the night, they can still hear moans and cries emanating from this area, as departed spirits continue to suffer barbaric operations.

THE PLAGUE HOUSE

In the small town of Hillsborough, there is a rural thoroughfare known as Bear Hill Road. For its own part, it is relatively unprepossessing and quiet. It does, however, harbor some otherworldly entities, which should be addressed.

There is a small, overgrown cemetery on this road, abandoned and largely forgotten. It is said that a spirit known as the "White Ghost" haunts this area, manifesting itself at sunset.

That the spirits should be restless here shouldn't come as any surprise; nearby the burial ground, located on private property, is an old cellar hole. This is all that remains of the infamous "Plague House" of the nineteenth century, where victims of disease were quarantined away from the general community. When these unfortunates passed away, they were buried deep in the woods so that animals could not get at them and spread the virus.

Actually, the kinds of diseases that could be spread during this time were nothing to sneeze at. It will be remembered that a tuberculosis epidemic in New England in the mid-nineteenth century led to the infamous vampire scare of that period. The earliest of these was the case of the Jewett City vampires of Connecticut. The illness fell on the Ray family in 1845, first killing twenty-four-year-old Lemuel and then his father, Henry B. Ray, in 1849. Other family members quickly succumbed to the disease, and their mutilated bodies were interred in the town cemetery. Then again, most of us are aware of the tale of Mercy Brown of Exeter, whose family quickly followed her to the grave. As her brother was seriously ill, the townspeople dug up Mercy's body, tore out her heart, burned it on a tree stump and then simmered it into a broth. They then fed this to the patient. Predictably, he died. This, however, did nothing to allay their superstitious fears.

Were the townspeople of Hillsborough assailed by similar trepidations? Is that why they buried the corpses deep in the forest, where they couldn't attack their neighbors? That we might never know. However, visitors to the site these days report that they see strange blue and yellow lights around the area. It is also said that one interloper decided to trespass on the cellar hole and began shouting derogatory slurs into the night air. Immediately, he was attacked, and large scratch marks were found on his back.

A FINAL WORD

There is something peculiar about New Hampshire in its obsession with the paranormal. Although the people of the area seem reluctant to discuss their encounters with the spirits, it's quite obvious something is going on. The towns that, during the daytime, are picture-postcard images of serenity and homeliness take on an entirely different aspect at night. You can sense that the spirits rest uneasily here, eager to tell their stories or wandering around with unfinished business. The cemeteries and old houses are redolent with paranormal activity, and history hangs heavily over the land. If you stand outside at night and quietly listen, you can almost hear them speaking out. Those with an open mind will hear.

BIBLIOGRAPHY

Boston Herald, May 24, 1922; December 27, 1906.

Boston Journal, November 16, 1880.

Boston Record American, November 14, 1954.

Coltrain, Warren Robert, and George K. Wood. *The History of Francestown, N.H. from Its Earliest Settlement, April 1758 to 1891.* Nashua, NH: James H. Barker, Printer, 1895.

Concord Herald, February 24, 1790; May 25 1790.

Farmers Cabinet, December 7, 1845; May 12 1875; October 8, 1811.

Goodale, John H. *The History of Nashua.* Nashua, NH: Telegraph Publishing Company, 1885.

Gustavus, A.C. "The Nashua of Today." *Granite Monthly: A New Hampshire Magazine Devoted to History, Biography, Literature and State Progress*, 1902.

Hopkins, John Monson. Centennial Celebration Address, October 24, 1839. Peterborough Transcript Office, 1890.

Nelson, Elias, and George Bailey Loring. *A History of the Town of Dunstable.* Boston: Alfred Mudge & Son, 1877.

New Hampshire Gazette, September 24 1773.

New Hampshire Sentinel, March 15, 1866.

New York Herald, December 3, 1874.

Nylander, Robert Harrington. "The David Hubbard House, Hancock, New Hampshire." *Old-Time New England* 49, no. 175 (Winter 1959).

Pennsylvania Packet, June 4, 1790.

Portland Daily Press, July 12, 1871.

Ramsdell, George M. *History of Hillsborough.* Manchester, NH: John B. Clarke Company, 1885.

Smith, Albert, MD. *The History of the Town of Peterborough, Hillsborough County, New Hampshire.* Boston: George H. Ellis, 1908.

Spofford, Harriet E.P. *New England Legends.* Boston: James R. Osgood and Company, 1871.

Weekly Advocate, June 30, 1904.

About the Author

Eric Stanway is a writer, artist and musician with over three decades of experience. Born in Manchester, England, he traveled extensively throughout the United States during the 1960s. In the 1980s, he fronted the experimental musical troupe the Brain Trust. Later, he worked with FantaCo publications in Albany, New York, where he adapted a number of classic horror stories by such authors as Charles Dickens and Ambrose Bierce into graphic formats. This led to his collaboration with author Clive Barker on a series of graphic novels entitled *Night of the Living Dead: London*. He has worked as an editor at various newspapers, including the *Sentinel* and *Enterprise* of Fitchburg, Massachusetts, and the *Cabinet* of Milford, New Hampshire. He has also written sixteen books on New England history, including the biography of famed diva Madame Sherri. He resides in Fitzwilliam, New Hampshire, with his significant other, extended family and Duncan, his huge black cat.

Visit us at
www.historypress.net

This title is also available as an e-book